T3-BOV-130

WITHDRAWN

BRENDAN BEHAN:
AN ANNOTATED BIBLIOGRAPHY OF CRITICISM

By the same author

The Social and Cultural Setting of the 1890s
John Galsworthy the Dramatist
Comedy and Tragedy
Sean O'Casey: A Bibliography of Criticism
A Bibliography of Modern Irish Drama
Dissertations on Anglo-Irish Drama
The Sting and the Twinkle: Conversations with Sean O'Casey
J. M. Synge: A Bibliography of Criticism
Contemporary British Drama 1950–1976
J. M. Synge: Interviews and Recollections
W. B. Yeats: Interviews and Recollections
English Drama 1900–1950
Lady Gregory: Interviews and Recollections
Oscar Wilde: An Annotated Bibliography of Criticism
A Research Guide to Modern Irish Dramatists
Oscar Wilde: Interviews and Recollections
The Art of Brendan Behan

BRENDAN BEHAN

An Annotated Bibliography
of Criticism

E. H. Mikhail

BARNES & NOBLE
BOOKS
10 East 53d St., New York 10022
(a division of Harper & Row Publishers, Inc.)

© E H Mikhail 1980

All rights reserved. No part of this publication may be
reproduced or transmitted, in any form or by any means,
without permission

*First published 1980 in the U.K. and all other parts of the world
excluding the U.S.A. by*
THE MACMILLAN PRESS LTD
London and Basingstoke

First published in the U.S.A. 1980 by
HARPER & ROW PUBLISHERS INC.
BARNES & NOBLE IMPORT DIVISION

PR
6003
E417
Z78

British Library Cataloguing in Publication Data

Mikhail, Edward Halim
  Brendan Behan
  1. Behan, Brendan – Criticism and interpretation
  – Bibliography
  016.822'9'14   Z8086./

MACMILLAN ISBN 0–333–27822–4

BARNES & NOBLE ISBN 0 06 4948269
LCN 79–12337

Printed in Hong Kong

To Beatrice Behan

for her immense help

Contents

CONTENTS

Acknowledgements

I wish to express my gratitude to Mrs. Beatrice Behan, without whose generous help and continuous cooperation this book would never have taken its present shape. She has graciously placed her husband's material at my disposal and has patiently answered all my queries. Brendan Behan scholars will undoubtedly share my appreciation of her assistance.

At various stages I received useful information, comments, support, or assistance from Mr Alan Simpson; Mr Gabriel Fallon; Mr Rory Furlong; Professor Robert Hogan; Dr Olof Lagerlöf; Professor Heinz Kosok; Ms Marianne Levander; Dr. Colbert Kearney; Miss Deirdre McQuillan and Miss Mary O'Neill of the National Theatre Society, Dublin; Miss Kate Mackay and Mr Nicholas Hern of Eyre Methuen Ltd., London; Mr Seamus de Burca; Mr Desmond MacNamara; the Canadian Broadcasting Corporation; Mr Cathal Goulding; Miss Alice E. Einhorn of Doubleday Publishers; Mr Louis Burke; Mrs Teresa Monaghan; Mr Brian McCoy; Radio Telefis Eireann; Mr John O'Riordan; Mrs Sharon Murphy; Mr Michael Cormican; Mr Manus Canning; Mr Brian Price; Miss Wendy Johnson; and Mr John Bennett.

I am grateful to Miss Bea Ramtej for her usual skill in preparing the final typescript; to Mr Tim Farmiloe of the Macmillan Press Ltd. for his encouragement and interest; to the late Allan Aslett and his staff of the same firm for their help in seeing the book through the press.

Thanks are due to the University of Lethbridge for granting me a sabbatical leave, during which this work was completed.

It is also a pleasant duty to record my appreciation to the staff of the University of Lethbridge Library; the British Library, London; the Newspaper Library, Colindale; the National Library of Ireland, Dublin; Trinity College Library, Dublin; the Bibliothèque Nationale, Paris; the National Library, Ottawa; and the New York Public Library.

E. H. M.

Preface

Almost all the critical evaluations of Brendan Behan's achievement vitiate themselves in accepting biased popular judgements of the writer's personality. In recent years, however, Behan's stature has undergone novel if not radical alteration. Several full-length books have been written on his life or his writings, in addition to the large amount of material in periodicals. Dissertations have been, and are being, written on him, and his plays are consistently being revived. In years to come, therefore, people reading his works will want to know more about Behan the man than the evil tradition which his name will evoke. Hence the need for the present work.

There is no full-length critical bibliography of Brendan Behan. Nor are existing bibliographical aids comprehensive in their coverage of Behan criticism. Various periodical indexes, for example, never list the large number of interviews Behan gave during his life. The *Essay and General Index* includes some essays on Behan in books, but neither recollections of him in books of reminiscences, nor references to him in books on dramatic literature.

Another difficulty I have encountered is the vast amount of material that has been written on Behan. As a result of Behan's versatility as a writer in both English and Gaelic, his wide travels in both Europe and North America, his excessive drinking, and his popular personality, there has probably been more literature dealing with him than with any other contemporary writer who produced the same amount of work. Apart from the additional burden which this large number of items has put on me in deciding what to include and what to exclude, the entries I eventually decided to include – totalling some 2,000 – left me no alternative but to resort to the added task of annotations as the only way in which a reader can distinguish, for example, between the several items entitled 'Brendan Behan'. The annotations, however, are not evaluative, but descriptive and indicative of the content of the material they describe. A small number of items, though, have not been annotated; in these cases I felt that the title of the entry is indicative enough of its content. Most of the annotations fall generally under broad categories such as 'Critical assessment', 'Biography', 'Interview with Behan', 'Recollections of Behan', or the title of work with which the entry deals. The cut-off date is 1976, although some later items have been included.

'Review articles' posed another problem. While it is true that a large number of reviews of books on Behan are somewhat superficial and do not add much to our knowledge of this dramatist, this category as a whole should not be ignored. I have, therefore, decided to include all the known reviews, and have annotated them as 'review articles', meaning that they are reviews of books *on* Behan. Reviews of books *by* Behan are, of course, included in the appropriate section dealing with his works. For the convenience of the reader, however, most of these reviews of Behan's works are also included in the section dealing with periodical articles, but have annotations which simply indicate the work they deal with: for instance, *Borstal Boy*, *The Hostage*, or *The Quare Fellow*.

E. H. Mikhail

I. Bibliographies

Abstracts of English Studies (Boulder, Colorado: National Council of
Teachers of English, 1958 to the present). [Summaries of selected
articles in periodicals.]

Adelman, Irving, and Rita Dworkin, 'Brendan Behan', *Modern Drama;
A Checklist of Critical Literature on 20th Century Plays* (Metuchen,
New Jersey: The Scarecrow Press, 1967) p. 50. [Selected criticism
in books.]

American Doctoral Dissertations, Compiled for the Association of Research
Libraries (Ann Arbor, Michigan: University Microfilms, 1963 to
the present). Continuation of *Index to American Doctoral
Dissertations*, listed below.

The American Humanities Index (Troy, New York: The Whitston
Publishing Company, 1975 to the present). [Material in
periodicals not indexed elsewhere.]

Annual Bibliography of English Language and Literature (London: Modern
Humanities Research Association, 1920 to the present). [Criticism
in books and international periodicals.]

Bibliographic Index; A Cumulative Bibliography of Bibliographies (New
York: H. W. Wilson, 1937 to the present). [Bibliographies in
books and periodicals.]

Book Review Digest (New York: H. W. Wilson, 1906 to the present).
[An index to reviews in selected periodicals of books published in
the United States. Some excerpts are included.]

Book Review Index (Detroit, Michigan: Gale Research Company, 1965
to the present). [Reviews of books in periodicals.]

'Books by Brendan Behan', *The Hollins Critic* (Hollins College,
Virginia), II, No. 1 (February 1965) 7.

Boyle, Ted E., 'Selected Bibliography', *Brendan Behan* (New York:
Twayne Publishers, 1969) pp. 143–145. [Primary works and
selected criticism in books and periodicals.]

Breed, Paul F., and Florence M. Sniderman, 'Brendan Behan',
*Dramatic Criticism Index; A Bibliography of Commentaries on
Playwrights from Ibsen to the Avant-Garde* (Detroit, Michigan: Gale

Research Company, 1972) pp. 97–98. [Selected criticism in books
and periodicals.]

British Humanities Index (London: The Library Association, 1962 to the
present). Continuation of *Subject Index to Periodicals*, 1915–1961.
[Articles in selected world periodicals.]

Canadian Periodical Index (Ottawa: Canadian Library Association, 1938
to the present). [Articles in Canadian periodicals.]

Carpenter, Charles A., 'Modern Drama Studies: An Annual
Bibliography', *Modern Drama*, XVII, No. 1 (March 1974) to the
present. [Lists books and periodical articles.]

Chicorel, Marietta, (ed.), 'Brendan Behan', *Chicorel Theater Index to
Plays in Anthologies, Periodicals, Discs and Tapes*, Vol. 1 (New York:
Chicorel, 1970) p. 38. [*The New House* and *The Quare Fellow*]; Vol.
2 (New York: Chicorel, 1971) p. 37. [*The Hostage* and *The Quare
Fellow*.]

——, (ed.), 'Brendan Behan', *Chicorel Theater Index to Plays in
Anthologies and Collections, 1970–1976*. (New York: Chicorel, 1976)
p. 36 [*The Quare Fellow*.]

Coleman, Arthur, and Gary R. Tyler, 'Brendan Behan', *Drama
Criticism Volume One: A Checklist of Interpretation Since 1940 of English
and American Plays* (Denver: Alan Swallow, 1966) p. 30. [Selected
criticism in books and periodicals.]

Connor, John M., and Billie M. Connor, 'Brendan Behan', *Ottemiller's
Index to Plays in Collections; An Author and Title Index to Plays
Appearing in Collections Published between 1900 and Early 1975*, 6th ed.,
rev. and enl. (Metuchen, New Jersey: The Scarecrow Press, 1976)
p. 29. [*The Hostage, The New House*, and *The Quare Fellow*.]

Dissertation Abstracts (Ann Arbor, Michigan: University Microfilms,
1938 to the present). [Abstracts of dissertations submitted to
American universities.]

Enser, A. G. S., *Filmed Books and Plays; A List of Books and Plays from
Which Films Have Been Made, 1928–1967*. Revised Edition (London:
Andre Deutsch, 1971) p. 201. [*The Quare Fellow*.]

Essay and General Literature Index (New York: H. W. Wilson, 1900 to the
present). [Essays in books.]

Etudes Irlandaises (Lille, France, 1972 to the present). [Annual survey of
research in France. Includes a section on Behan.]

Fidell, Estelle A. (ed.), *Play Index, 1953–1960; An Index to 4592 Plays in
1735 Volumes* (New York: H. W. Wilson, 1963) p. 24 [*The Hostage
and The Quare Fellow*]; *Play Index, 1961–1967; An Index to 4793 Plays*
(New York: H. W. Wilson, 1968) p. 25 [*The Hostage* and *The*

Quare Fellow]; *Play Index, 1968–1972; An Index to 3848 Plays* (New
York: H. W. Wilson, 1973) p. 22. [*Borstal Boy* and *The New
House.*]
Gerdes, Peter René, *The Major Works of Brendan Behan*. European
University Papers, Series XIV, Vol. 10 (Bern: Herbert Lang;
Frankfurt: Peter Lang, 1973) pp. 253–255 [Works by Behan];
p. 256. [Selected criticism on Behan.]
Guide to the Performing Arts (New York: The Scarecrow Press, 1957 to
the present). [Selected articles in periodicals.]
Haskell, John D., Jr., and Robert G. Shedd, 'Modern Drama: A
Selective Bibliography of Works Published in English', *Modern
Drama*, X, No. 2 (September 1967) 210. [Selected criticism in
books and periodicals.]
Havlice, Patricia Pate, 'Brendan Behan', *Index to Literary Biography*,
Vol. I (Metuchen, New Jersey: Scarecrow Press, 1975) p. 95. [A
quick reference tool for locating biographical information.]
Hayes, Richard J. (ed.), 'Brendan Behan', *Sources for the History of Irish
Civilisation: Articles in Irish Periodicals 1940–1967, Vol. 1* (Boston: G.
K. Hall, 1970) p. 193. [Selected criticism.]
Holden, David F., 'Brendan Behan', *An Analytical Index to Modern
Drama, Volumes I–XIII, May 1958–February 1971* (Toronto:
Hakkert, 1972) p. 14. [Articles on Behan published in *Modern
Drama*.]
Howard, Patsy C., ed. 'Brendan Behan', *Theses in English Literature
1894–1970* (Ann Arbor, Michigan: The Pierian Press, 1973) p. 14.
[M. A. theses in American universities.]
Index to American Doctoral Dissertations (New York: H. W. Wilson, 1955
to the present).
An Index to Book Reviews in the Humanities (Williamston, Michigan:
Phillip Thomson, 1961 to the present). [Lists reviews in
English.]
Index to Little Magazines, 1960–1961 (Denver, Colorado: Alan Swallow,
1962) p. 17. [*The Big House* in *Evergreen Review*.]
International Association for the Study of Anglo-Irish Literature.
'Bibliography Bulletin', *Irish University Review; A Journal of Irish
Studies* (Dublin, 1972 to the present). [Includes a section on Behan
studies.]
International Index to Periodicals (New York: H. W. Wilson, 1907 to the
present). From volume 19 (April 1965–March 1966) called *Social
Sciences and Humanities Index*. From April 1974 called *Humanities
Index*. [Articles in selected world periodicals.]

Junge, Ewald, 'World Drama on Records', *Theatre Research*, VI, No. 1
    (1964) 18. [*The Quare Fellow*.]

Keller, Dean H., *Index to Plays in Periodicals* (Metuchen, New Jersey:
    Scarecrow Press, 1971) pp. 46–47. [*The Big House, The Hostage*,
    and *The Quare Fellow*.]

Kersnowski, Frank L., C. W. Spinks, and Laird Loomis. 'Brendan
    Behan', *A Bibliography of Modern Irish and Anglo-Irish Literature* (San
    Antonio, Texas: Trinity University Press, 1976) pp. 4–5. [Primary
    works and selected criticism in books.]

Mellown, Elgin W. 'Brendan Behan', *A Descriptive Catalogue of the
    Bibliographies of 20th Century British Poets, Novelists, and Dramatists*,
    2nd. Ed., rev. and enl. (Troy, New York: Whitston Publishing
    Company, 1978) p. 21. [Primary and secondary bibliographies.]

Mersand, Joseph, ed. 'Brendan Behan', *Guide to Play Selection; A
    Selective Bibliography for Production and Study of Modern Plays*, 3rd ed.
    (Urbana, Illinois: National Council of Teachers of English; New
    York: R. R. Bowker, 1975) p. 84. [*The Hostage*.]

Mikhail, E. H. 'A Select Bibliography', *Brendan Behan: The Complete
    Plays* (London: Eyre Methuen, 1978), pp. 28–34. [Criticism in
    books and periodicals.]

———, 'Brendan Behan', *A Research Guide to Modern Irish Dramatists*
    (Troy, New York: Whitston Pub. Co., 1979) pp. 4–5 [Annotated
    bibliography of bibliographies.]

MLA Bibliography (New York: The Modern Language Association of
    America, 1919 to the present). [Criticism in books and
    periodicals.]

The New York Directory of the Theater (New York: Arno Press, 1973)
    p. 67. [Material on Behan and the theatre in *The New York
    Times*.]

The New York Times Index, 1913 to the present. [Material on Behan in
    The New York Times.]

Palmer, Helen H., and Anne Jane Dyson, 'Brendan Behan', *European
    Drama Criticism* (Hamden, Connecticut: The Shoe String Press,
    1968) pp. 47–48; *Supplement I* (Hamden, Connecticut: The Shoe
    String Press, 1970) p. 20; *Supplement II* (Hamden, Connecticut:
    The Shoe String Press, 1974) p. 14. [Selected criticism in books
    and periodicals.]

Patterson, Charlotte A., comp. *Plays in Periodicals: An Index to English
    Language Scripts in Twentieth Century Journals* (Boston,
    Massachusetts: G. K. Hall, 1970) p. 65. [*The Hostage*.]

Porter, Raymond J., 'Selected Bibliography', *Brendan Behan*. Columbia

Essays on Modern Writers 66 (New York and London: Columbia
University Press, 1973) p. 48. [Principal works and selected
criticism.]

Pownall, David E., 'Brendan Behan', *Articles on Twentieth Century
Literature: An Annotated Bibliography 1954–1970* (Millwood, New
York: Kraus-Thomson, 1973) p. 201. [Selected articles in
periodicals, with annotations.]

Readers' Guide to Periodical Literature (New York: H. W. Wilson, 1900 to
the present). [Articles in periodicals published in the United
States.]

Roach, Helen, *Spoken Records*. 3rd. Ed. (Metuchen, New Jersey: The
Scarecrow Press, 1970) pp. 139–140. [*The Quare Fellow* and *The
Hostage*.]

Royal Irish Academy, The Committee for the Study of Anglo-Irish
Language and Literature. *Handlist of Work in progress* (Dublin,
1969 to the present). [Includes a section on Behan.]

Royal Irish Academy, The Committee for the Study of Anglo-Irish
Language and Literature. *Handlist of Theses Completed But Not
Published* (Dublin, 1973 to the present). [Includes a section on
Behan.]

Saddlemyer, Ann, 'Brendan Behan', *English Drama (excluding
Shakespeare); Select Bibliographical Guides*, ed. Stanley Wells
(London: Oxford University Press, 1975) p. 258. [Plays and
selected criticism in books.]

Sader, Marion, (ed.) 'Brendan Behan', *Comprehensive Index to English-
Language Little Magazines, 1890–1970*, vol. 1 (Millwood, New York:
Kraus-Thomson, 1976) p. 287. [Selected criticism in little
magazines.]

Salem, James M., 'Brendan Behan', *A Guide to Critical Reviews, Part III:
British and Continental Drama from Ibsen to Pinter* (Metuchen, New
Jersey: The Scarecrow Press, 1968) pp. 34–35. [Selected criticism
in periodicals.]

Samples, Gordon, 'Brendan Behan', *The Drama Scholars' Index to Plays
and Filmscripts: A Guide to Plays in Selected Anthologies, Series and
Periodicals* (Metuchen, New Jersey: The Scarecrow Press, 1974)
p. 33. [*The Big House, The Hostage, and The Quare Fellow*.]

Schoolcraft, Ralph Newman, 'Brendan Behan', *Performing Arts Books in
Print: An Annotated Bibliography* (New York: Drama Book
Specialists, 1973) pp. 205–206. [Selected books on Behan.]

Sharp, Harold S., and Marjorie Z. Sharp (comps.), *Index to Characters
in the Performing Arts; An Alphabetical Listing of 30,000 Characters*.

Part I: Non-Musical Plays, 2 vols. (Metuchen, New Jersey: The
Scarecrow Press, 1966). [Characters identified with the play in
which they appear.]

Shedd, Robert G., Modern Drama: A Selective Bibliography of Works
Published in English', *Modern Drama*, V, No. 2 (September
1962)–IX, No. 2 (September 1966). [Lists books and periodical
articles.]

Social Sciences and Humanities Index (New York: H. W. Wilson), 1965 to
the present. Continuation of *International Index to Periodicals*. From
April 1974 called *Humanities Index*. [Articles in selected world
periodicals.]

Subject Index to Periodicals (London: The Library Association, 1915–
1961). Continued as *British Humanities Index*, (1962 to the present).
[Articles in selected world periodicals.]

Temple, Ruth Z., and Martin Tucker, (eds.) 'Brendan Behan',
Twentieth Century British Literature; A Reference Guide and Bibliography
(New York: Frederick Ungar, 1968) pp. 133–134. [Primary
books.]

The Times Index (London, 1790 to the present). [Material on Behan in
The Times.]

The Times Literary Supplement Index (London, 1902 to the present).
[Material on Behan in *The Times Literary Supplement*.]

Trussler, Simon, 'Current Bibliography', *Theatre Quarterly* (London,
1971–1973). Continued in *Theatrefacts; International Theatre
Reference* (London, 1974 to the present). [Lists new books.]

Twentieth Century Literature, (1955 to the present). [Contains a regular
quarterly selected annotated 'Current Bibliography'.]

Year's Work in English Studies (London: The English Association, 1919
to the present). [Annotated selective bibliography.]

II. Published Books by Behan and their Reviews

THE QUARE FELLOW [Play]

A) English edition (London: Methuen, 1956). Reviewed by Adrian
Mitchell in *The London Magazine*, IV, No. 8 (August 1957) 77–79;
in *The Irish Times* (Dublin, 17 November 1956) p. 6; by A. J.
L[eventhal] in *The Dublin Magazine*, XXXII (January–March
1957) 52–53; and by Liam Miller in *Irish Writing* (Dublin), No.
36 (Autumn–Winter 1956) 189–190.

B) American edition (New York: Grove Press, 1957). Reviewed in
Time (Chicago), LXX (29 July 1957) 82; in *Booklist* (Chicago),
LIV (1 November 1957) 132; in *Atlantic Monthly* (Boston), CC
(October 1957) 180–181; and by Norman K. Dorn in *San
Francisco Chronicle*, (25 August 1957) p. 23.

BORSTAL BOY [Autobiographical novel]

A) English edition (London: Hutchinson, 1958). Reviewed in *The
Times* (London, 30 October 1958) p. 13; by Gerard Fay in *The
Manchester Guardian*, (21 October 1958) p. 4; by Kenneth Allsop in
Daily Mail (London, 18 October 1958) p. 4; by John Gritten in
Daily Worker (London, 23 October 1958) p. 2; by W. J. Randall
in *The Catholic Herald* (London, 21 November 1958) p. 3; in *The
Times Literary Supplement*, (24 October 1958) p. 606; by Cyril
Connolly in *The Sunday Times* (London, 19 October 1958) p. 17;
by Maurice Richardson in *The Observer* (London, 19 October
1958) p. 21; by Christopher Logue in *New Statesman* (London),
LVI (25 October 1958) 566–567; by Donat O'Donnell in *The
Spectator* (London, 7 November 1958) p. 620; in *The Listener*

(London), LX (6 November 1958) 743; by Peregrine Walker in
The Tablet (London, 25 October 1958) 360–361; by Cathal O
Dubh in *The Irish Democrat* (London, October 1958) 7; by Brian
Glanville in *Reynolds News* (London, 19 October 1958) p. 6;
by W. G. S. in *Books and Bookmen* (London), IV (November
1958) 13; by Hugh Delargy in *Tribune* (London, 24 October
1958) p. 10; by Martin Sheridan in *The Irish Times* (Dublin, 25
October 1958) p. 6; by Philip Rooney in *The Irish Press* (Dublin,
25 October 1958) p. 4; by Cathal O'Shannon in *Evening Press*
(Dublin, 24 October 1958) pp. 10, 14; and by Risteárd Ó Glaisne
in *Focus; A Monthly Review* (Belfast), I, No. 11 (November 1958)
44–45.

B) American edition (New York: Alfred A. Knopf, 1959). Reviewed
by Orville Prescott in *The New York Times*, (27 February 1959)
p. 23; by John Wain in *New York Times Book Review*, (22 February
1959) p. 1; by Donald Malcolm in *New Yorker*, XXXV, No. 20 (4
July 1959) 69–72; by Riley Hughes in *The Catholic World* (New
York), CLXXXIX (May 1959) 165–166; by Frank O'Connor in
Chicago Sunday Tribune, (1 March 1959) p. 3; by Thomas F.
Curley in *The Commonweal* (New York), LXIX (13 March 1959)
628–629; in *Kirkus Reviews* (New York), XXVI (15 December
1958) 936; by Earle F. Wallbridge in *Library Journal* (New York),
LXXXIV (15 March 1959) 844; by W. S. Merwin in *The Nation*
(New York), CLXXXIII (28 February 1959) 190–191; by John
K. Hutchens in *New York Herald Tribune*, (23 February 1959) p.
11; by Gene Baro in *New York Herald Tribune Book Review*, (22
February 1959) p. 5; by A. M. Sullivan in *Saturday Review* (New
York), XLII (28 February 1959) 35; in *Newsweek*, LIII (23
February 1959) 105–106; in *Time* (Chicago), LXXIII (9 March
1959) 86–87; by Donovan Bess in *San Francisco Chronicle*, (8 March
1959) p. 16; by Alfred Kazin in *Atlantic Monthly* (Boston), CCIII
(June 1959), 65–67 [Reprinted in his *Contemporaries* (Boston:
Little, Brown, 1962) pp. 240–246]; by Otto Friedrich in *The
Reporter* (New York), XX (19 March 1959) 45–46; by Steven
Marcus in *Partisan Review*, XXVI, No. 2 (Spring 1959) 335–344;
by Edith Fowke in *Canadian Forum*, XXXIX (May 1959) 44; by
Olivier Todd in *France Observateur* (Paris, 22 December 1960) 21;
and by Maurice Nadeau in *L'Express* (Paris, 22 December 1960)
pp. 29–30.

THE HOSTAGE [Play]

A) English edition (London: Methuen, 1958). Reviewed [briefly] in
   The Times Literary Supplement (London, 19 December 1958)
   p. 743; by Charles Osborne in *The London Magazine*, VI
   (September 1959) 90; by Conor O'Brien in *The Tablet* (London, 7
   February 1959) 133–134; by Edith Shackleton in *The Lady*
   (London), CXLIX (22 January 1959) 116; by Thomas Kilroy in
   Studies; An Irish Quarterly Review (Dublin), XLVIII (Spring 1959)
   111–112; and by Risteárd Ó Glaisne in *Focus; A Monthly Review*
   (Belfast), II (February 1959) 28–29.

B) American edition (New York: Grove Press, 1959).

C) Gaelic edition [*an Giall*] (Baile Átha Cliath: An Chomhairle
   Náisiúnta Drámaíochta, n.d.).

BRENDAN BEHAN'S ISLAND; AN IRISH SKETCH-
BOOK. With Drawings by Paul Hogarth [Tape-recorded
impressions]

A) English edition (London: Hutchinson, 1962). Reviewed in *The
   Times Literary Supplement*, (12 October 1962) p. 791; by Louis
   MacNeice in *The Observer* (London, 30 September 1962) p. 29; by
   Cyril Connolly in *The Sunday Times* (London, 30 September 1962)
   p. 32; by Nigel Dennis in *The Sunday Telegraph* (London, 30
   September 1962) p. 6; by Robert Greacen in *The Listener*
   (London), LXVIII (4 October 1962) p. 527–529; by Gerard Fay
   in *The Spectator* (London, 5 October 1962) p. 528; by W. R.
   Rodgers in *New Statesman* (London), LXIV (12 October 1962)
   492; in *The Economist* (London, 3 November 1962) 479–480; by B.
   C. L. Keelan in *The Tablet* (London, 13 October 1962) 960; by
   R. W.-E. in *Books and Bookmen* (London, October 1962) 39; by T.
   Redmond in *The Irish Democrat* (London, January 1963) 7; by
   Owen Edwards in *Tribune* (London, 5 October 1962) p. 10; by
   Violet Powell in *Punch* (London, 17 October 1962) 576; by
   Terence de Vere White in *The Irish Times* (Dublin, 29 September
   1962) p. 8; by F. J. Keane in *Irish Independent* (Dublin, 13 October
   1962) p. 10; by Don MacAlernon in *Focus; A Monthly Review*
   (Belfast), V (December 1962) 283; and by F. McE. in *The*

Kilkenny Magazine, No. 9 (Spring 1963) 85–87.

B) American edition (New York: Bernard Geis, 1962). Reviewed by
Charles Poore in *The New York Times*, (23 October 1962) p. 35;
by Anne O'Neill-Barna in *The New York Times Book Review*, (4
November 1962) p. 5; by Michael Campbell in *Saturday Review*
(New York), XLV (3 November 1962) 48; by John F. Moran in
Library Journal (New York), LXXXVII (15 December 1962)
4541; by Patricia MacManus in *New York Herald Tribune Books*, (7
July 1963) p. 6; by James T. McCartin in *The Reporter* (New
York), XXVIII (31 January 1963) 56; by Haskel Frankel in *Show*
(New York), II (January 1963) 36; by Archer Finch in *Book-of-
the-Month-Club News* (New York, January 1963) 12; by Clifton
Fadiman in *Holiday* (Philadelphia), XXXIII (April 1963), 20; in
Albany Times-Union (Albany, New York, 11 November 1962)
p. H6; by Richard Ellmann in *Chicago Sunday Tribune Magazine of
Books*, (4 November 1962) p. 2; by Rita Fitzpatrick in *Chicago
Sunday Times*, (16 November 1962); in *The Sunday Star*
(Washington, D.C., 11 November 1962) p. B5; by William Hogan
in *San Francisco Chronicle*, (1 November 1962) p. 35; by S. K.
Oberbeck in *St. Louis Post Dispatch* (Missouri, 14 October 1962)
p. 4B; by T. M. in *The Houston Chronicle*, (21 October 1962) p. 15;
by Charles Poore in *St. Petersburg Times* (Florida, 4 November
1962) p. 15; by Thad Stem, Jr. in *Charlotte Observer* (North
Carolina, 28 October 1962) p. 5E; by John De Witt McKee in
Sun Dial (El Paso, Texas, 28 October 1962); by Robert J. Thomas
in *Rutland Daily Herald* (Vermont, 23 October 1962) p. 8; by F. P.
Jackman in *Worcester Sunday Telegram*, (4 November 1962) p. 10E;
by Larry Walker in *Oklahoman* (Oklahoma City, Oklahoma, 30
December 1962) p. 3D; by Howard Schultz in *Richmond Times
Dispatch* (Virginia, 18 November 1962) p. L11; in *Sunday Herald
Leader* (Kentucky, 30 December 1962) p. 25; by Martha B.
McCoy in *Chattanooga Times* (Tennessee, 2 December 1962); by
Madge Wilson in *Daily Press* (Virginia, 2 December 1962) p. 4D;
by Van Allen Bradley in *Long Island Press* (25 November 1962)
Section 7, p. 9; by Harold L. Cail in *Portland Evening Express*
(Maine, 28 November 1962) p. 16; by James Haddican in *The
Times-Picayune* (New Orleans, 25 November 1962) Section 4,
p. 14; by Mary O'Hara in *Pittsburgh Press*, (21 October 1962)
Section 5, p. 10; by James Nolan in *Newark News*, (18 November
1962) Section 4, p. 14; by John H. O'Brien in *Detroit News*

(Michigan, 18 November 1962) p. 3G; by Bernard Kelly in
Denver Post, (4 December 1962) p. 23; by Francis J. Thompson in
Tampa Tribune, (13 January 1963); by Arnold Powell in
Birmingham News (Alabama, 25 November 1962) p. E-7; and by
John Barkham in *The Vancouver Sun* (14 November 1962) p. 5.

HOLD YOUR HOUR AND HAVE ANOTHER. With Decorations
by Beatrice Behan [A collection of the best columns Behan wrote for
the *Irish Press*, 1954–1956]

A) English edition (London: Hutchinson, 1963). Reviewed in *The
Times* (London, 26 September 1963) p. 15; in *The Times Literary
Supplement* (27 September 1963) p. 774; by D. A. N. Jones in *New
Statesman* (London), LXVI (4 October 1963) 450; by Brian Inglis
in *The Spectator* (London, 1 November 1963) 566; by W. R.
Rodgers in *The Sunday Times* (London, 15 September 1963) p. 30;
by Robert Greacen in *The Listener* (London), LXIX (3 October
1963) 516; by B. C. L. Keelan in *The Tablet* (London), CCXVII
(23 November 1963) 1268; by A. Hamilton in *Books and Bookmen*
(London), X (June 1965) 41; by Ignotus in *The Irish Democrat*
(London, December 1963) 7; by Owen Edwards in *Tribune*
(London, 25 October 1963) p. 9; by Edith Shackleton in *The Lady*
(London), CLVIII (26 September 1963) 418; by Maurice
Kennedy in *The Irish Times* (Dublin, 14 September 1963) p. 8; by
Don MacAlernon in *Focus; A Monthly Review* (Belfast), VI
(November 1963) 262; and by T. H. in *The Kilkenny Magazine*,
No. 10 (Autumn–Winter 1963) 121–122.

B) American edition (Boston: Little, Brown, 1964). Reviewed by
Charles Poore in *The New York Times*, (28 January 1964) p. 29;
by Anne O'Neill-Barna in *The New York Times Book Review*, (2
February 1964) p. 7; by Christopher Ricks in *New York Review of
Books*, II (30 July 1964) pp. 8–9; by Alan Pryce-Jones in *New
York Herald Tribune*, (28 January 1964) p. 19; by Jimmy Breslin in
New York Herald Tribune, (2 February 1964) pp. 5, 21; in *New
Yorker*, XL (14 March 1964) 191; in *Newsweek* (New York),
LXIII (3 February 1964) 82–83; by A. M. Sullivan in *Saturday
Review* (New York), XLVII (8 February 1964) 39–40; by John F.
Moran in *Library Journal* (New York), LXXXIX (15 January
1964) 259; by Paul Gavaghan in *America* (New York), CX (22

February 1964) 261; by Jimmy Breslin in *Book Week* (New York, 2 February 1964) pp. 5, 21; by Stephen P. Ryan in *The Critic* (Chicago), XXII (February 1964) 80; by Stephen P. Ryan in *Best Sellers* (Scranton, Pennsylvania), XXIII (1 February 1964) 383; and by William Barrett in *Atlantic Monthly* (Boston), CCXIII (February 1964) 143.

THE SCARPERER [The book form of the novel which was first published as a serial in *The Irish Times* in 1953 under the pseudonym of 'Emmet Street'].

A) American edition (Garden City, New York: Doubleday, 1964). Reviewed by Charles Poore in *The New York Times*, (23 June 1964) p. 31; by Anne O'Neill-Barna in *New York Times Book Review*, (21 June 1964) p. 5; by Christopher Ricks in *New York Review of Books*, II (30 July 1964) pp. 8–9; by Emile Capouya in *Saturday Review* (New York), XLVII (20 June 1964) 36–37; by Thomas F. Curley in *Commentary* (New York), XXXVIII (August 1964) 70–71; by Edward Boyle in *Book-of-the-Month-Club News* (New York, August 1964) 12; by Lloyd W. Griffin in *Library Journal* (New York), LXXXIX (15 June 1964) 2640; in *Library Journal* (New York), LXXXIX (15 September 1964) 3504; by Brian Moore in *Book Week (New York Herald Tribune*, 21 June 1964) pp. 3, 14; in *Newsweek* (New York), LXIII (29 June 1964) 89; in *New Yorker*, XL (1 August 1964) 78; by W. B. Hill in *America* (New York), CXI (28 November 1964) 718–719; by Paul Levine in *Hudson Review*, XVII (Autumn 1964) 470–477; in *Prairie Schooner*, XXXIX, No. 2 (Summer 1965) 175; in *Time* (Chicago), LXXXIII (19 June 1964) 96; by Richard Sullivan in *Books Today (Chicago Tribune*, 21 June 1964) p. 6; by Connolly Cole in *Chicago Daily News*, (27 June 1964) p. 8; by Horace Reynolds in *The Christian Science Monitor* (Boston, 18 June 1964) p. 7; by Stephen P. Ryan in *Best Sellers* (Scranton, Pennsylvania), XXIV (1 July 1964) 137; by William Barrett in *Atlantic Monthly* (Boston), CCXIV (July 1964) 139; by Rick Anderson in *Sunday Olympian* (Washington, D.C., 28 June 1964) p. 5; in *Sunday Star* (Washington, D.C., 21 April 1964) p. C5; by Bernard Kelly in *The Sunday Denver Post*, (5 July 1964) p. 10; in *The Sioux City Sunday Journal*, (12 July 1964) p. C4; by John Haase in *Los Angeles Times*, (12 July 1964) p. 15; by John H. O'Brien in *The Detroit*

News, (7 June 1964) p. 3G; by Ann F. Wolfe in *Columbus Dispatch* (Ohio, 5 July 1964) p. 12; by T. H. in *Providence Sunday Journal* (Rhode Island, 12 July 1964) p. U-18; by Jack A. Rye in *Sacramento Bee*, (5 July 1964) p. 16; in *The Sunday Oregonian* (Portland, Oregon, 12 July 1964) p. 43; by Brock Lucas in *St. Petersburg Times* (Florida, 28 June 1964) p. 5; by Connolly Cole in *Buffalo Evening News*, (11 July 1964) p. B-10; in *Sunday Call-Chronicle* (Allentown, Pennsylvania, 5 July 1964) p. B-9; and by Victor Paul Hass in *Omaha World-Herald*, (28 June 1964) p. 27.

B) English edition (London: Hutchinson, 1966). Reviewed in *The Times* (London, 1 December 1966) p. 16; in *The Times Literary Supplement*, (24 November 1966), p. 1104; by Stephen Fay in *The Sunday Times* (London, 13 November 1966) p. 28; by Norman Shrapnel in *Manchester Guardian Weekly*, (24 November 1966) p. 11; by Desmond MacNamara in *New Statesman* (London), LXXII (18 November 1966) 750; by Colin MacInnes in *The Observer* (London, 13 November 1966) p. 26; by Isabel Quigly in *The Spectator* (London), CCXVII (18 November 1966) 657; by Hilary Corke in *The Listener* (London), LXXVI (1 December 1966) 819; by John Moynihan in *The Sunday Telegraph* (London, 13 November 1966) p. 15; in *Books and Bookmen* (London), XII (February 1967) 57; by B. A. Young in *Punch* (London), CCLII (4 January 1967) 31; by Jack White in *The Irish Times* (Dublin, 12 November 1966) p. 8; by Ronan Farren in *Irish Independent* (Dublin, 19 November 1966) p. 10; by Augustine Martin in *The Irish Press* (Dublin, 12 November 1966) p. 6; in *Evening Herald* (Dublin, 25 November 1966) p. 14; by Eamon Grennan in *The Dublin Magazine*, VI (Spring 1967) 97–98; by Liam O Luanaigh in *Inniu* (Dublin, 14 April 1967) p. 2; and by Seán McMahon in *Eire-Ireland* (St. Paul, Minnesota), I, No. 4 (Winter 1966) 97–98.

BRENDAN BEHAN'S NEW YORK. With Drawings by Paul Hogarth [More tape-recorded impressions]

A) English edition (London: Hutchinson, 1964). Reviewed in *The Times Literary Supplement*, (22 October 1964) p. 955; by D. A. N. Jones in *New Statesman* (London), LXVIII (9 October 1964) 544; by Louise W. King in *The Sunday Times* (London, 27 September 1964) p. 48; by Lord Kinross in *The Sunday Telegraph* (London, 27

September 1964) p. 22; by E. S[tevens] in *Books and Bookmen* (London), X (January 1965) 27; in *The Economist* (London), CCXIII (14 November 1964) 720; by T. R[edmond] in *The Irish Democrat* (London, February 1965) 7; in *The Observer* (London, 6 November 1966) p. 22 [Corgi paperback edition]; by Fergus Linehan in *The Irish Times* (Dublin, 24 October 1964) p. 8; and by Donagh MacDonagh in *The Kilkenny Magazine*, Nos. 12–13 (Spring 1965) 55–60.

B) American edition (New York: Bernard Geis, 1964). Reviewed by Anne O'Neill-Barna in *New York Times Book Review*, (15 November 1964) p. 6; by John Barkham in *New York World-Telegram and Sun*, (10 November 1964) p. 63; by Jessie Kitching in *New York Post*, (8 November 1964) p. 47; by John F. Moran in *Library Journal* (New York), LXXXIX (1 December 1964) 4802; by William Barrett in *Atlantic Monthly* (Boston), CCXV (January 1965) 130; in *Best Sellers* (Scranton, Pennsylvania), XXIV (1 November 1964) 306; by M. A. M[alkin] in *Antiquarian Bookman*, XXXVI (6 September 1965) 813; in *Booklist* (Chicago), LXI (1 December 1964) 335; by Robert Cromie in *Chicago Tribune*, (16 November 1964) Section 2, p. 2; by T. R. in *Chicago Daily News*, (7 November 1964); in *Catholic Standard* (Washington, D.C., 20 November 1964) p. 9; by Carl Winston in *San Francisco News Call Bulletin*, (7 November 1964) p. 7; by George Block in *Tulsa World*, (6 December 1964); by P. S. in *The Fayette Observer*, (8 November 1964) p. 5D; by Jonathan M. Klarfeld in *Holyoke Transcript-Telegram* (Massachusetts, 14 November 1964) p. 12; by George Roberts in *Columbus Citizen-Journal* (Ohio, 7 November 1964) Section 2, p. 1; by Tom Gray in *Columbus Enquirer* (Ohio, 28 December 1964) p. 8; by Maie E. Perley in *The Louisville Times*, (19 November 1964) Section 1, p. 13; in *Clearwater Sun*, (8 November 1964) p. 8-D; by Don Hatfield in *Huntington Herald-Dispatch*, (1 November 1964) p. 35; by Carl Gartner in *Des Moines Sunday Register*, (1 November 1964) p. 7F; by W. B. in *Plain Dealer* (Cleveland, Ohio, 29 November 1964) Section BB, p. 5; by Miles A. Smith in *Augusta Chronicle* (Georgia, 8 November 1964) p. 14E; by Richard B. Larsen in *The Atlanta Journal*, (8 November 1964) p. 12-D; by F. P. Jackman in *Worcester Sunday Telegram*, (8 November 1964) p. 10E; by James Haddican in *The Times-Picayune* (New Orleans, 20 December 1964); by R. F. H. in *Register-Mail* (Galesburg, Illinois, 19 November 1964); by

Franklin D. Cooley in *Richmond Times-Dispatch* (Virginia, 22
November 1964) p. L-11; by Alvin H. Goldstein in *St. Louis Post-
Dispatch* (Missouri, 6 December 1964) p. 3K; by George Near in
Herald Banner (Greenville, Texas, 22 November 1964) p. B2; by
James Powers in *Hollywood Reporter*, (27 November 1964) p. 5; by
L. E. in *Durhan Morning Herald*, (15 November 1964) p. 5D; by
Don Keown in *Independent-Journal* (San Rafael, California, 31
October 1964) p. M14; by Anne Sweeney in *Nashville Banner*, (18
December 1964); by Mary Chase in *Rocky Mountain News*
(Denver, Colorado, 8 November 1964) p. 20A; by Ronald S.
Ziemba in *The Springfield Republican*, (15 November 1964) p. 4D;
by Peter Kohler in *Charlotte Observer* (North Carolina, 22
November 1964) Section C, p. 2; and by Walter Spearman in
Rocky Mount Sunday Telegram (North Carolina, 6 December 1964)
p. 5B.

CONFESSIONS OF AN IRISH REBEL [More tape-recorded
impressions; posthumous sequel to *Borstal Boy*, covering the period
from Behan's release from Hollesley Bay until his marriage to
Beatrice in 1955]

A) English edition (London: Hutchinson, 1965). Reviewed in *The
Times Literary Supplement*, (11 November 1965) p. 995; by
Margaret Drabble in *The Sunday Times* (London, 31 October
1965) p. 52; by Patrick Anderson in *The Spectator* (London),
CCXV (19 November 1965) 665; by Maurice Richardson in *The
Observer* (London, 7 November 1965) p. 27; by Desmond
MacNamara in *New Statesman* (London), LXX (5 November
1965) 705; by W. J. White in *Manchester Guardian Weekly*, (18
November 1965) p. 10; by Elsie O'Dowling in *The Irish Democrat*
(London, December 1965) 7; by Barbara Trewick in *Books and
Bookmen* (London), XII (March 1967) 38; by Desmond Rushe in
Irish Independent (Dublin, 13 November 1965) p. 9; and by
Connolly Cole in *The Dublin Magazine*, V (Spring 1966) 95.

B) American edition (New York: Bernard Geis, 1966). Reviewed in
The New York Times, (25 April 1966) p. 28 [Advance notice]; by
Lewis Nichols in *New York Book Review*, (22 May 1966) p. 8; by
Seán O'Faoláin in *New York Times Book Review*, (26 June 1966)
p. 7; by Stanley Weintraub in *Saturday Review* (New York), IL (4
June 1966) 47; by Roderick W. Childers in *National Observer* (New

York), V (6 June 1966) 21; by Sean Cronin in *The Nation* (New
York), CCIII (7 November 1966) 486–488; by J. F. Moran in
Library Journal (New York), XCI (July 1966) 3402; in *Kirkus
Reviews*, XXXIV (1 February 1966) 153; by Stephen P. Ryan in
Best Sellers (Scranton, Pennsylvania), XXVI (1 June 1966) 94; in
Antiquarian Bookman, XXXVII (3 January 1966) 13; by Stanley
Weintraub in *Books Abroad*, XLI (1967) 227–228; in *Time*
(Chicago), LXXXVII (3 June 1966) 98; in *Booklist*, LXIII (1
February 1967) 559; in *Publishers' Weekly* (Philadelphia), CXCII
(30 October 1967) 53; in *Choice*, IV (June 1967) 418; by David
McCullough in *Book-of-the-Month-Club News*, (May 1966) 10; by
Charles Richman in *Brooklyn Record*, (6 May 1966); in *The Sunday
Post Tribune*, (8 May 1966); by James E. Alexander in *Pittsburgh
Post Gazette & Sun Telegraph*, (21 May 1966); by Ralph Bergamo
in *Atlanta Journal Constitution*, (15 May 1966); by John K.
Sherman in *Minneapolis Sunday Tribune* (22 May 1966) Section E,
p. 6; by Phil Millf in *Pensacola Journal*, (22 May 1966); by Gynter
Quill in *Waco Tribune Herald*, (28 May 1966) p. 11A; by Don
Keown in *Independent Journal* (San Rafael, California, 28 May
1966); by Frank Rahill in *Milwaukee Journal*, (15 May 1966) part
5, p. 4; by Roy Newquist in *Chicago's American*, (29 May 1966); in
Heights Star (Chicago, 29 May 1966) p. 10; by George Near in
The Greenville Herald Banner (Texas, 12 April 1966) p. B2; by
Brendan Malin in *Boston Globe*, (26 June 1966) p. A24; by Donald
Freeman in *The San Diego Union*, (3 July 1966) p. E6; by Alice
McKenzie in *Clearwater Sun* (Florida, 29 May 1966) p. 7-D; by
Bonita Sparrow in *Memphis Commercial Appeal*, (19 June 1966)
Section 5, p. 8; by James Allen in *Miami News*, (19 June 1966)
p. 17; by Francis J. Thompson in *The Tampa Tribune*, (3 July
1966) p. 31; by Carl Costella in *Duluth News Tribune* (Minnesota,
5 June 1966) Cosmopolitan Section, p. 2; in *Catholic Standard*
(Washington, D.C., 9 June 1966); by Sherry Kafka Coughley in
Morning Star-Telegram (Forth Worth, Texas, 26 June 1966); by
C. A. B. in *Buffalo News*, (25 June 1966); by Jim Higly in *Buffalo
Courier-Express*, (3 July 1966) Section D, p. 8; by James
Retherford in *The Indianapolis Star*, (24 July 1966) Section 7, p. 5;
by Goldie Capers Smith in *Tulsa Sunday World*, (10 July 1966)
p. 15; by Nat Honig in *Press Telegram* (Long Beach, California, 3
August 1966) p. A 33; in *Lake Charles American Press*, (16 July
1966) p. 6; by Zoe Brockman in *Gastonia Gazette* (North Carolina,
31 July 1966); by M. M. in *People's World* (San Francisco, 27

August 1966); by James Quinlan in *Pitts-Burgh Catholic*, (23
November 1966) p. 5; in *The Rocky Mount Telegram* (North
Carolina, 4 September 1966); by Bernard Kelly in *Denver Post*
(Colorado, 5 September 1966) p. 25; by Jan M. Dyroff in *Patriot
Ledger* (Quincy, Massachusetts, 10 August 1966) p. 36; and by Ed
Mauel in *Sunday Press-Enterprise* (Riverside, California, 4
September 1966) p. C-10.

MOVING OUT AND A GARDEN PARTY. TWO PLAYS OF
BRENDAN BEHAN. Introduced by Micheál Ó hAodha. Edited by
Robert Hogan. The 'Short Play' Series, No. 3 (Dixon, California:
Proscenium Press, 1967). [Based on the happenings of the Behan
household.]

RICHARD'S CORK LEG, ed. with Additional Material by Alan
Simpson [Play].

A) English edition (London: Eyre Methuen, 1973). Reviewed in *The
   Times Literary Supplement*, (26 April 1974) p. 440; by Romilly
   Cavan in *Plays and Players* (London), XXI (November 1973) 71;
   in *Books and Bookmen* (London), XIX (October 1973) 140; in *The
   Amateur Stage* (London), XXVIII (November 1973) 50; in *British
   Book News* (London, November 1973) 761; and by J. J. Finegan
   in *Evening Herald* (Dublin, 3 November 1973) p. 11.

B) American edition (New York: Grove Press, 1973).

III. Criticism on Brendan Behan

A) Books

Anderson, Garrett, *Brennan's Book* (Edinburgh: Paul Harris, 1977).
  [The Author's Note to this novel advises us that 'one of the main
  characters behaves in some ways as one of the main characters in
  Dublin did in those days'.]
Armstrong, William A., 'The Irish Point of View: The Plays of Sean
  O'Casey, Brendan Behan, and Thomas Murphy', *Experimental
  Drama* (London: G. Bell, 1963) pp. 79–102.
——, 'The Irish Dramatic Movement', *Classic Irish Drama*
  (Harmondsworth, Middlesex: Penguin, 1964) pp. 7–15 passim.
Aspler, Tony, *The Streets of Askelon* (London: Secker & Warburg,
  1971). [A novel based loosely on Behan's appearance at McGill
  University, Montreal.]
Atkinson, Brooks, 'The Behan', *Tuesdays and Fridays* (New York:
  Random House, 1963) pp. 19–21. Reprinted from *The New York
  Times* (9 December 1960) p. 28 [Interview with Behan.]
Behan, Beatrice, *My Life with Brendan*. With Des Hickey and Gus
  Smith (London: Leslie Frewin, 1973; Los Angeles: Nash, 1974).
  [Recollections of Behan by his widow.]
'Behan, Brendan', *McGraw-Hill Encyclopedia of World Drama, Volume I*
  (New York: McGraw-Hill, 1972) pp. 165–169.
Behan, Brian, *With Breast Expanded* (London: MacGibbon & Kee,
  1964). [Autobiography by Brendan's brother. Chapter 30 is on
  Brendan.]
Behan, Dominic, *Teems of Times and Happy Returns* (London:
  Heinemann, 1961). American edition entitled *Tell Dublin I Miss
  Her* (New York: G. P. Putnam, 1962). [Autobiography of
  Brendan's brother.]
——, *My Brother Brendan* (London: Leslie Frewin, 1965; New York:
  Simon and Schuster, 1966). [Biography.]

18

Bell, J. Bowyer. *The Secret Army* (London: Blond; New York: John
  Day, 1970), passim. [Behan and the Irish Republican Army.]
Bergner, Heinz, 'Brendan Behan: *The Hostage* (1958)', *Das
  zeitgenössische englische Drama: Einführung, Interpretation,
  Dokumentation*, ed. Klaus-Dieter Fehse and Norbert H. Platz
  (Frankfurt: Athenäum, 1975) pp. 86–100. [A study of the play; in
  German.]
Blum, Daniel, (ed.), '*The Quare Fellow*', *Theatre World, Season 1958–1959*
  (Philadelphia: Chilton Company, 1959) p. 145. [At the Circle in
  the Square Theatre, New York.]
——, (ed.), 'Brendan Behan', *Theatre World, Season 1963–1964*
  (Philadelphia: Chilton Company, 1964) p. 254. [Obituary.]
Böll, Heinrich, 'Brendan Behan', *Aufsätze-Kritiken-Reden* (Köln and
  Berlin: Kiepenheuer & Witsch, 1967) pp. 189–192. Reprinted in
  Missing Persons and Other Essays. Translated from the German by
  Leila Vennewitz (London: Secker & Warburg, 1977) pp. 98–102.
  [Reflections on Behan as a man and 'personality'.]
Borel, Françoise, 'Alas, Poor Brendan!', *Aspects of the Irish Theatre*.
  Cahiers Irlandais 1, ed. Patrick Rafroidi, Raymonde Popot, and
  William Parker (Paris: Editions Universitairs, Publications de
  l'Université de Lille, 1972) pp. 119–136. [*The Hostage* and *The
  Quare Fellow*.]
Boylan, Henry, 'Brendan Behan', *A Dictionary of Irish Biography*
  (Dublin: Gill and Macmillan, 1978) p. 22.
Boyle, Ted E., *Brendan Behan* (New York: Twayne Publishers, 1969).
  [Biography and criticism.]
'Brendan Behan', *Obituaries from the Times 1961–1970* (Reading,
  England: Newspaper Archive Development Limited) pp. 64–65.
  Reprinted from *The Times* (London, 21 March 1964) p. 12.
Brockett, Oscar G. 'English Theatre and Drama Since 1945', *History of
  the Theatre* (Boston: Allyn and Bacon, 1968) pp. 675–676. [*The
  Hostage* and *The Quare Fellow*.]
Brockett, Oscar G., and Robert R. Findlay, *Century of Innovation: A
  History of European and American Theater and Drama Since 1870*
  (Englewood Cliffs, New Jersey: Prentice-Hall, 1973) pp. 621–622.
  [*The Hostage* and *The Quare Fellow*.]
Brustein, Robert. 'Libido at Large: *The Hostage* by Brendan Behan',
  Seasons of Discontent; Dramatic Opinions 1959–1965 (New York:
  Simon & Schuster, 1965; London: Jonathan Cape, 1966) pp.
  177–180.
——, 'Two Plays about Ireland', *The Culture Watch; Essays on Theatre*

and Society 1969–1974 (New York: Alfred A. Knopf, 1975) pp. 53–
54. [*Richard's Cork Leg.*]
Burgess, Anthony, 'The Writer As Drunk', *Urgent Copy; Literary Studies*
(New York: W. W. Norton, 1968; London: Jonathan Cape, 1969)
pp. 88–92. Reprinted from *The Spectator* (London), CCXVII (4
November 1966), 588. [Review article.]
Claudel, Paul-Henri, 'Note liminaire du traducteur', *Brendan Behan:
Encore un verre avant de partir* (Paris: Gallimard, 1970) pp. 7–8.
[Introduction to the French translation of *Hold Your Hour and Have
Another.*]
Clurman, Harold, 'Introduction', *Seven Plays of the Modern Theater*
(New York: Grove Press, 1962) pp. vii–xii. [*The Quare Fellow.*]
——, 'Brendan Behan: *The Hostage*, 1960', *The Naked Image;
Observations on the Modern Theatre* (New York: Macmillan; London:
Collier-Macmillan, 1966) pp. 43–44.
Connery, Donald S., *The Irish* (London: Eyre & Spottiswoode,
1968) pp. 189–190 and passim. [Behan and the Irish
background.]
Coogan, Timothy Patrick, *Ireland Since the Rising* (New York: Frederick
A. Praeger, 1966) passim. [Behan as a writer.]
——, *The Irish; A Personal View* (London: Phaidon Press, 1975) passim.
[Behan as a writer].
Corsani, Mary, *Il Nuovo Teotro Inglese* (Milan: U. Mursia, 1970) pp.
176–178. [*The Hostage* and *The Quare Fellow.*]
Costello, Peter, *The Heart Grown Brutal: The Irish Revolution in Literature,
from Parnell to the Death of Yeats, 1891–1939* (Dublin: Gill and
Macmillan; Totowa, New Jersey: Rowman and Littlefield, 1977)
pp. 295–296 [*Borstal Boy, The Hostage,* and *The Quare Fellow*] and
passim.
Cronin, Anthony. *Dead As Doornails; A Chronicle of Life* (Dublin:
Dolmen Press; London: Calger & Boyars, 1976) passim.
[Recollections of Behan.]
Deale, Kenneth E. L., *Memorable Irish Trials* (London: Constable,
1960) chapter VI. [An account of the trial of Bernard Kirwan,
who was the original 'Quare Fellow'.]
DeBurca, Seamus, *The Soldier's Song: The Story of Peadar Kearney*, 2nd
ed. (Dublin: P. J. Bourke, 1958). [A biography of Behan's uncle,
the author of Ireland's National Anthem. Includes some
references to Behan's mother.]
——, *Brendan Behan; A Memoir*. The Proscenium Chap-books, No. 1
(Newark, Delaware: Proscenium Press, 1971).

——, *Down to the Sea in a Tanker* (Dublin: P. J. Bourke, 1972). [A reprint of an article referred to by Behan in a letter to his cousin Seamus DeBurca written from Mountjoy Prison in 1943.

Donleavy, J. P., *The Ginger Man* (New York: Delacorte Press, 1965) passim.

Drescher, Horst W., 'The Drama', *World Literature Since 1945*, ed. Ivar Ivask and Gero von Wilpert (New York: Frederick Ungar, 1973) p. 102. [Brief introduction.]

Drury, F. K. W., 'Brendan Behan', *Drury's Guide to Best Plays*, by James M. Salem (Metuchen, New Jersey: The Scarecrow Press, 1969) p. 47. [Synopses of *The Hostage* and *The Quare Fellow*.]

Duprey, Richard A., *Just Off the Aisle; The Ramblings of a Catholic Critic* (Westminster, Maryland: Newman Press, 1962) pp. 83–91. [*The Hostage* and *The Quare Fellow*.]

Edwards, Hilton, 'The Irish Theatre', *A History of the Theatre*, by George Freedley and John A. Reeves, 3rd rev. ed. (New York: Crown Publishers, 1968) pp. 735–749 passim.

Evans, Sir Ifor, *A Short History of English Drama*. Second Edition (Boston: Houghton Mifflin, 1965) pp. 205–206. [*The Hostage* and *The Quare Fellow*.]

Fallis, Richard, *The Irish Renaissance* (Syracuse, New York: Syracuse University Press, 1977) pp. 268–270 [Evaluation of Behan as a writer.]

'Feicreanach'. *Who Killed Brendan Behan?* (London: [Connolly Association], n.d.). [A 12-page pamphlet in defence of Behan reprinted from *The Irish Democrat*, May 1964.]

Flanner, Janêt [Genet], *Paris Journal 1944–1965*, ed. William Shawn (New York: Atheneum, 1965) p. 417. [*The Hostage*.]

Foley, Donal, *Three Villages: An Autobiography* (Dublin: Egotist Press, 1977) pp. 79–80. [Recollections of Behan.]

Forbes-Robertson, Diana, and André van Gyseghem, 'England (1955–1965)', *A History of the Theatre*, by George Freedley and John A. Reeves, 3rd rev. ed. (New York: Crown Publishers, 1968) pp. 728–735 passim.

Freyer, Grattan, ed. *Modern Irish Writing* (Dublin: Irish Humanities Centre, 1978). [Anthology including the text of, and a commentary on, *The Big House*.]

Fricker, Robert. *Das Moderne Englische Drama* (Göttingen: Vandenhoeck and Ruprecht, 1974) pp. 155–156. [*The Hostage* and *The Quare Fellow*.]

Gascoigne, Bamber, *Twentieth-Century Drama* (London: Hutchinson

University Library, 1962) pp. 200–202. [*The Quare Fellow* and *The Hostage.*]

Gerdes, Peter René. *The Major Works of Brendan Behan.* European University Papers, Series XIV, Vol. 10 (Bern: Herbert Lang; Frankfurt: Peter Lang, 1973). [Studies of *The Quare Fellow*, *Borstal Boy*, *An Giall*, and *The Hostage.*]

Gilliatt, Penelope. '*The Hostage*', *The Encore Reader; A Chronicle of the New Drama*, ed. Charles Marowitz, Tom Milne, and Owen Hale (London: Methuen 1965), pp. 94–95. Reprinted from *Encore* (London), V, No. 4 (November 1958) 35–36.

Goetsch, Paul, 'Das Gesellschaftsdrama seit Shaw', *Das Englische Drama*, ed. Josefa Nünning (Darmstadt: Wissenschaftliche Buchgesellschaft, 1973) pp. 429–430 [*The Hostage*]; p. 438 [*The Quare Fellow.*]

Gozenpud, A., *Puti i pereput'ya. Angliiskaya i frantsuzskaya dramaturgiya XXV* [Roads and Cross-Roads. English and French 20th Century Drama] (Leningrad: Iskusstvo, 1967) pp. 159–162. [*The Quare Fellow* and *The Hostage.*]

Gray, Tony, *Gone the Time* (London: Heinemann, 1967) [A novel in which the hero, Fogarty, is a poet modelled closely on Behan in his last years.]

Guernsey, Otis L., Jr. (ed.), *The Best Plays of 1964–1965* (New York: Dodd, Mead, 1965) pp. 53–54. [*The Hostage.*]

—— (ed.), *The Best Plays of 1965–66* (New York: Dodd, Mead, 1966) p. 82. [*The Hostage.*]

—— (ed.), *The Best Plays of 1966–1967* (New York: Dodd, Mead, 1967) pp. 86–87, 98, 422. [*The Hostage.*]

—— (ed.), *The Best Plays of 1967–1968* (New York: Dodd, Mead, 1968) pp. 64–65, 75. [*The Hostage.*]

—— (ed.), *The Best Plays of 1968–69* (New York: Dodd, Mead, 1969) p. 127. [*The Hostage.*]

—— (ed.), *The Best Plays of 1969–1970* (New York: Dodd, Mead, 1970) pp. 14–15, 324 [*Borstal Boy*]; pp. 56, 61–62 [*The Hostage.*]

—— (ed.), *The Best Plays of 1970–1971* (New York: Dodd, Mead, 1971) p. 80 [*The Hostage*]; p. 288 [*Borstal Boy.*]

—— (ed.), *The Best Plays of 1971–1972* (New York: Dodd, Mead, 1972) pp. 91–104. [*The Hostage.*]

—— (ed.), *The Best Plays of 1972–1973* (New York: Dodd, Mead, 1973) pp. 24, 62, 78, 375 [*The Hostage*]; p. 63 [*Borstal Boy*]; pp. 100, 118, 122 [*Richard's Cork Leg*]; p. 390 [*Shay Duffin as Brendan Behan.*]

—— (ed.), *The Best Plays of 1973–1974* (New York: Dodd, Mead, 1974), p. 50 [*The Hostage.*]

—— (ed.), *The Best Plays of 1974–1975* (New York: Dodd, Mead, 1975) pp. 51, 82 [*The Hostage.*]

—— (ed.), *The Best Plays of 1975–1976* (New York: Dodd, Mead, 1976) p. 81 [*The Hostage*]; p. 370 [*Conversations with an Irish Rascal*, adapted from the works of Behan.]

—— (ed.), *The Best Plays of 1976–1977* (New York: Dodd, Mead, 1977) pp. 59–60 [*The Hostage.*]

—— (ed.), *The Best Plays of 1977–1978* (New York: Dodd, Mead, 1978) pp. 86–87, 136. [*The Hostage.*]

Guerrero Zamora, Juan, *Historia del teatro contemporaneo*, vol. IV (Barcelona: Juan Flors, 1967) pp. 41–42. [*The Quare Fellow* and *The Hostage.*]

Hale, John (ed.), *Post-War Drama: Extracts from Eleven Plays* (London: Faber, 1966). [Includes an extract from, and commentary on, *The Quare Fellow.*]

Heiney, Donald, and Lenthiel H. Downs, 'Brendan Behan', *Contemporary British Literature* (Woodbury, New York: Barron's Educational Series, 1974) pp. 140–142. [Introductory essay.]

Hewes, Henry (ed.), *The Best Plays of 1961–1962* (New York: Dodd, Mead, 1962) pp. 29, 33, 315–316. [*The Hostage.*]

—— (ed.), *The Best Plays of 1962–1963* (New York: Dodd, Mead, 1963) pp. 43, 48. [*The Hostage.*]

—— (ed.), *The Best Plays of 1963–1964* (New York: Dodd, Mead, 1964) pp. 38, 48. [*The Hostage.*]

Hinchcliffe, Arnold P., *British Theatre 1950–70* (Oxford: Basil Blackwell, 1974) pp. 52–53. [*The Hostage* and *The Quare Fellow.*]

Hogan, Robert, 'The Short Happy World of Brendan Behan', *After the Irish Renaissance; A Critical History of the Irish Drama Since 'The Plough and the Stars'* (Minneapolis: University of Minnesota Press, 1967) pp. 198–207.

Hortmann, Wilhelm, 'Theatre Workshop: Behan', *Englische Literatur im 20. Jahrhundert* (Bern and München: A. Francke, 1965) pp. 175–176. [*The Quare Fellow* and *The Hostage.*]

Jeffs, Rae, 'Afterword', *Brendan Behan: The Scarperer* (New York: Doubleday, 1964) pp. 157–158. British edition entitled 'Foreword', *Brendan Behan: The Scarperer* (London: Hutchinson, 1966) pp. 5–7. [Recollections of Behan.]

——, 'Preface', *Brendan Behan: Confessions of an Irish Rebel* (London: Hutchinson, 1965) pp. 7–12; American edition entitled

'Foreword', *Brendan Behan: Confessions of an Irish Rebel* (New York: Bernard Geis, 1966) pp. vii–x. [Recollections of Behan.]

——, *Brendan Behan: Man and Showman* (London: Hutchinson, 1966; Corgi edition, 1968; New York: World Publishing, 1968). [The pleasure and pain of Behan's company detailed by the editor of the tape-recorded books. Covers the period 1957 to Behan's death.]

Jordan, John, 'The Irish Theatre – Retrospect and Premonition', *Contemporary Theatre*. Stratford-upon-Avon Studies 4, ed. John Russell Brown and Bernard Harris (London: Edward Arnold, 1968) pp. 180–181. [*The Quare Fellow* and *The Hostage*.]

Joyce, C. A., *By Courtesy of the Criminal; The Human Approach of the Treatment of Crime* (London: George G. Harrap, 1955). [Background recollections by the former governor of Hollesley Bay Borstal, where Behan was jailed.]

Kazin, Alfred, 'Brendan Behan: The Causes Go, the Rebels Remain', *Contemporaries* (Boston: Little, Brown, 1962) pp. 240–246. Reprinted from *Atlantic Monthly*, CCIII (June 1959) 65–67. [*Borstal Boy*.]

Kearney, Colbert, *The Writings of Brendan Behan* (Dublin: Gill and Macmillan, 1977). [The first complete study of Behan's works.]

Kearney, Peadar, *My Dear Eva: Letters from Ballykinlar Internment Camp 1921*. Introduced by Seamus DeBurca (Dublin: P. J. Bourke, 1976). [Letters by Behan's uncle to his wife, including references to Kathleen Behan, Brendan's mother.]

Kenny, Herbert A., *Literary Dublin; A History* (New York: Taplinger; Dublin: Gill & Macmillan, 1974) pp. 239–240; 283–289. [Behan as a writer.]

Kerr, Walter, *The Theater in Spite of Itself* (New York: Simon & Schuster, 1963) pp. 108–112 [*The Hostage*.]

Kiely, Benedict, 'That Old Triangle: A Memory of Brendan Behan', *The Sounder Few: Essays from the 'Hollins Critic'*, ed. R. H. W. Dillard, George Garrett, and John R. Moore (Athens, Georgia: University of Georgia Press, 1971) pp. 85–99. Reprinted from *The Hollins Critic* (Hollins College, Virginia), II, No. 1 (February 1965) 1–12.

Kienzle, Siegfried, 'Brendan Behan', *Modern World Theater; A Guide to Productions in Europe and the United States Since 1945*. Translated by Alexander and Elizabeth Henderson (New York: Frederick Ungar, 1970) pp. 55–57. [Synopses of *The Big House*, *The Hostage* and *The Quare Fellow*.]

Kitchin, Laurence, *Mid-Century Drama* (London: Faber and Faber, 1960) pp. 23–24, 110–111. [*The Hostage.*]

Kosok, Heinz, 'Brendan Behan: *The Hostage*', *Das englische Drama der Gegenwart; Interpretationen*, ed. Horst Oppel (Berlin: Erich Schmidt, 1976) pp. 30–48.

Kronenberger, Louis (ed.), *The Best Plays of 1960–1961* (New York: Dodd, Mead, 1961) pp. 12–14, 51–69, 295 [*The Hostage.*]

Lennartz, Franz (ed.), 'Brendan Behan', *Ausländische Dichter und Schriftsteller unserer Zeit*, 4th rev. ed. (Stuttgart: Kröner, 1971) pp. 93–95. [Introductory essay.]

Lorda Alaiz, F. M., 'Continuación de la tradición dramática irlandesa: Los Behan', *Teatro ingles: De Osborne hasta hoy* (Madrid: Taurus, 1964) pp. 151–160. [Behan as a continuation of the Irish dramatic tradition.]

Lumley, Frederick, *New Trends in 20th Century Drama; A Survey Since Ibsen and Shaw* (London: Barrie and Rochliff, 1960) pp. 303–304. [*The Quare Fellow* and *The Hostage.*]

MacAnna, Tomas, 'Nationalism from the Abbey Stage', *Theatre and Nationalism in Twentieth-Century Ireland*, ed. Robert O'Driscoll (Totonto: University of Toronto Press, 1971) pp. 89–101.

McCann, Sean (ed.), *The World of Brendan Behan* (London: The New English Library, 1965; New York: Twayne Publishers, 1966). [Contents: Jimmy Hiney, 'The Ballad of Brendan Behan'; 'The Things that Brendan Said'; Sean McCann, 'Brendan Behan – A New Look'; Anthony Butler, 'Growing Up'; Marion Fitzgerald, 'His Parents'; Anthony Butler, 'The Rebel'; John Murdoch, 'Borstal and Money'; Sean Kavanagh, 'In Prison'; Marion Fitzgerald, 'His Wife'; Mary Lodge, 'His First Play'; Kevin Sullivan, 'The Last Playboy of the Western World'; Benedict Kiely, 'The Old Triangle'; Kevin Casey, 'The Raw and the Honest – A Critical Look'; Fred O'Donovan and Ken Stewart, 'Meet the Quare Fella'; Francis MacManus, 'The Broadcaster'; Anthony Butler, 'The Catacombs'; Terry O'Sullivan, 'His Dublin Haunts'; Donal Foley, 'His London Appearances'; Liam Dwyer, 'Just One Day'; Gabriel Fallon, 'Rite Words in Rote Order'; Catherine Rynne, 'The Behan We Knew'; John B. Keane, 'A Last Instalment'; and Micheál MacLiammóir, 'The Importance of Being Brendan'.]

—— (comp.), 'Introduction', *The Wit of Brendan Behan* (London: Leslie Frewin, 1968) pp. 7–10.

MacLiammóir, Micheál, *Theatre in Dublin* (Dublin: Published for the
    Cultural Relations Committee of Ireland at the Three Candles,
    1964). [Behan is 'the most stirring and certainly the most
    sensational of new discoveries made by the Irish Stage in the
    'fifties'.]
McMahon, Frank, *Brendan Behan's Borstal Boy; Adapted for the Stage*
    (Dublin: Four Masters; New York: Random House, 1971).
Matlaw, Myron, 'Brendan Behan', *Modern World Drama; An
    Encyclopedia* (London: Secker & Warburg, 1972) pp. 70–71.
Milne, Tom, and Clive Goodwin, 'Working with Joan', *Theatre at
    Work: Playwrights and Productions in the Modern British Theatre*, ed.
    Charles Marowitz and Simon Trussler (London: Methuen, 1967)
    pp. 113–122. [*The Hostage* and *The Quare Fellow*.]
Natev, Atanas, *Sovremenna zapadna dramaturgiya* [Contemporary Western
    Drama] (Sofia: Nauka i Jskustvo, 1965) pp. 247, 401–403. [Behan
    and the Theatre of the Absurd.]
Nicoll, Allardyce, 'Irish Epilogue', *World Drama from Aeschylus to
    Anouilh*. Revised and Enlarged Edition (London: Harrap, 1976)
    pp. 818–820. [Critical assessment.]
Nooteboom, Cees, 'Nawood', *Brendan Behan: De man van morgen; De
    gijzelaar* (Amsterdam: Uitgeverij de Bezige bij, 1965) pp. 169–172.
    [Epilogue to the Dutch translation of *The Quare Fellow* and *The
    Hostage*.]
Norman, Frank, *Why Fings Went West* (London: Lemon Tree Press,
    1975) passim. [Behan and the drama of the 1950s.]
O'Brien, Conor Cruise, *Writers and Politics* (New York: Pantheon
    Books, 1965) pp. 126–127. [Behan's attitude towards England and
    her prison system as revealed in *Borstal Boy*.]
O'Connor, Ulick, *Brendan Behan* (London: Hamish Hamilton, 1970;
    Englewood Cliffs, New Jersey: Prentice-Hall, 1971; rpt. London:
    Coronet Books, 1972). [Biography.]
——, *The Bailey; The Story of a Famous Tavern* (Dublin: The Bailey,
    n.d.) pp. 18–19, 26. [Where Behan was a customer.]
Ó hAodha, Micheál, 'Introduction', *Moving Out and a Garden Party.
    Two Plays by Brendan Behan*, ed. Robert Hogan. The 'Short Play'
    Series (Dixon, California: Proscenium Press, 1967) pp. 3–6.
——, 'Brendan Behan', *The Abbey – Then and Now* (Dublin: The Abbey
    Theatre, 1969) pp. 69–77.
——, *Theatre in Ireland* (Oxford: Basil Blackwell; Totowa, New Jersey:
    Rowman and Littlefield, 1974) pp. 141–148. [*The Hostage,
    The Quare Fellow, Moving Out, A Garden Party*, and *The Big House*.]

Pasquier, Marie-Claire, Nicole Rougier and Bernard Brugière, 'Joan Littlewood', *Le nouveau théâtre anglais* (Paris: Armand Colin, 1969) pp. 44–46. [*The Quare Fellow* and *The Hostage*.]

Petersen, Hans, 'Nachbemerkung', *Brendan Behan: Der Spanner* (Berlin: Volk und Welt, 1969) pp. 152–154. [Epilogue to the German edition of *The Scarperer*.]

Popkin, Henry (ed.), *The New British Drama* (New York: Grove Press, 1964). [Includes *The Hostage*.]

Porter, Raymond J., *Brendan Behan*. Columbia Essays on Modern Writers (New York and London: Columbia University Press, 1973). [Criticism.]

Quinn, Edward, 'Brendan Behan', *The Reader's Encyclopedia of World Drama*, ed. John Gassner and Edward Quinn (New York: Thomas Y. Crowell, 1969) p. 58.

Richards, Stanley (ed.), *Best Short Plays of the World Theatre 1958–1967* (New York: Crown Publishers, 1968) pp. 17–35. [Includes *The New House*, with a commentary.]

—— (ed.), *The Tony Winners* (Garden City, New York: Doubleday, 1977). [Includes *Borstal Boy*, adapted for the stage by Frank McMahon.]

Rudman, Harry W., and Irving Rosenthal (eds.), *A Contemporary Reader; Essays for Today and Tomorrow* (New York: Ronald Press, 1961) pp. 332–335. [Extract from *Confessions of an Irish Rebel*, with a commentary.]

Ryan, John, 'The Home and Colonial Boy', *Remembering How We Stood; Bohemian Dublin at the Mid-Century* (Dublin: Gill and Macmillan, 1975) pp. 61–79. [Recollections of Behan.]

Salem, Daniel, 'Brendan Behan (1923–1964)', *La Révolution Théâtrale Actuelle en Angleterre* (Paris: Denoel, 1969) pp. 78–82. [*The Quare Fellow* and *The Hostage*.]

Sarukhîan, Alla Pavlovna, *Sovremennaîa Irlandskaîa Literatura* [Contemporary Irish Literature] (Moskeva: Izdatel 'stvo Nauka, 1973) pp. 28–30. [General criticism.]

Schafer, Jürgen, 'Brendan Behan', *Englische Literatur der Gegenwart in Einzeldarstellungen*, ed. Horst W. Drescher (Stuttgart: Alfred Kröner, 1970) pp. 493–512. [Critical survey and bibliography.]

Shank, Theodore J. (ed.), '*The Hostage*', *A Digest of 500 Plays; Plot Outlines and Production Notes* (New York: Collier Books; London: Collier Macmillan, 1966) p. 411.

Sheehy, Michael, *Is Ireland Dying? Culture and the Church in Modern Ireland* (London: Hollis & Carter, 1968) pp. 112–115. [*The Hostage*.]

Shestakov, D. *Sovremennaya angliyskaya drama (Osbornoucy)*
[Contemporary English Drama (The Followers of Osborne)]
(Moscow: Vysshaya Shkola, 1968) pp. 22–26. [*The Hostage*.]
— (ed.), *Sem' angliĭskikh p'es* [Seven English Plays] Moscow:
Iskusstvo, 1968) [*The Hostage*.]
Simpson, Alan, *Beckett and Behan and a Theatre in Dublin* (London:
Routledge and Kegan Paul, 1962; New York: Hillary House,
1966). [*The Quare Fellow* at the Pike Theatre.]
Simpson Alan, 'Behan: The Last Laugh', *A Paler Shade of Green*, by Des
Hickey and Gus Smith (London: Leslie Frewin, 1972) pp. 209–219.
[Recollections of Behan.]
——, 'Introduction', *Brendan Behan: Richard's Cork Leg* (London: Eyre
Methuen, 1973; New York: Grove Press, 1974) pp. 5–11.
——, 'Introduction', *Brendan Behan: The Complete Plays* (London: Eyre
Methuen, 1978) pp. 7–25.
Sofinskû, V. 'Irlandskû Myatezhnik [Irish Rebel]', *Sovremennaya
literatura zarubezhom* [Contemporary Literature Abroad]. (Moscow:
Sovyetsku Pisately, 1975) pp. 174–186. [Behan as a writer and as
a freedom fighter].
Sprinchorn, Evert (ed.), 'Brendan Behan: *The Hostage*', *20th-Century
Plays in Synopsis* (New York: Thomas Y. Crowell, 1965) pp. 64–66.
Stanford, Derek (ed.), 'Brendan Behan', *Landmarks* (London and
Camden, New Jersey: Thomas Nelson, 1969) pp. 91–97. [Excerpt
from, and commentary on, *The Quare Fellow*.]
Taylor, John Russell, 'Brendan Behan', *Anger and After; A Guide to the
New British Drama*. 2nd. ed., (London: Methuen, 1969) pp. 123–
130. [*The Quare Fellow* and *The Hostage*.]
Temple, Ruth Z., and Martin Tucker (eds.), 'Brendan Behan', *A
Library of Literary Criticism; Modern British Literature* (New York:
Frederick Ungar, 1966) pp. 58–59. [Excerpts from criticism on
Behan.]
Tracy, Robert, 'Ireland: The Patriot Game', *The Cry of Home: Cultural
Nationalism and the Modern Writer*, ed. E. Ernest Lewald
(Knoxville, Tennessee: University of Tennessee Press, 1972) pp.
39–57. [Nationalism in Behan's works.]
Trewin, J. C., *Drama in Britain 1951–1964* (London: Longmans, Green
for the British Council, 1965) pp. 29–30. [*The Quare Fellow* and
The Hostage.]
Tynan, Kenneth, *Curtains* (New York: Atheneum, 1961) pp. 136–138
[*The Quare Fellow*]; pp. 218–220, 235–236 [*The Hostage*].
Reprinted in *A View of the English Stage 1944–63* (London: Davis-

Poynter, 1975) pp. 179–181 and pp. 225–228, respectively.

Wallechinsky, David, et al., *The Book of Lists* (New York: William Morrow, 1977) p. 338. [Behan listed among 56 male 'renowned homosexuals and bisexuals'.]

Weise, Wolf-Dietrich, *Die 'Neuen englischen Dramatiker' in inhrem Verhältnis zu Brecht* (Bad Homburg: Gehlen, 1969) pp. 66–74. [*The Quare Fellow* and *The Hostage.*]

Wellwarth, George, 'Brendan Behan: The Irish Primitive', *The Theater of Protest and Paradox; Developments in Avant-Garde Drama* (New York: New York University Press, 1964) pp. 258–261. [*The Quare Fellow* and *The Hostage.*]

White, Terence de Vere. *Ireland* (London: Thames & Hudson, 1968) passim.

Willis, John (ed.), *'Borstal Boy', Theatre World; 1969–1970 Season* (New York: Crown Publishers, 1970) p. 49. [At the Lyceum Theatre, New York.]

B) Periodical Articles

'Abbey Director's Spirited Defence of Brendan Behan', *The Sunday Independent* (Dublin, 29 January 1961) p. 5 [Gabriel Fallon champions Behan at a debate in Dublin.]

Abirached, Robert, 'Le Théâtre dans la Cité: Aristophane, Calderon, Behan', *Études*, (April 1962) 99–103. [Behan as a dramatist.]

Adams, Cindy, 'Brendan Behan: Ireland's Stormiest Writer', *The Pittsburgh Press* (3 November 1963) p. 24. Also as 'A Visit with the Behans', *The Philadelphia Inquirer Magazine*, (3 November 1963) 16. [Interview with Behan.]

Alexander, James E., 'Behan "Confesses"', *Pittsburgh Post Gazette & Sun Telegraph*, (21 May 1966). [*Confessions of an Irish Rebel.*]

Alldridge, John, 'Behan Takes Swallow – But Won't Touch the Bait', *Manchester Evening News*, (21 December 1961) p. 3. [Interview with Behan.]

Allen, James, 'Behan's Farewell', *Miami News* (19 June 1966) p. 17. [*Confessions of an Irish Rebel.*]

Allsop, Kenneth, 'His New Play Is Loaded', *The Irish Digest* (Dublin), LIX, No. 1 (March 1957) 31–32. [Interview with Behan.]

——'It's a Bomb of a Book by Behan', *Daily Mail* (London, 18 October 1958) p. 4. [*Borstal Boy.*]

——, 'Behan Bestows an Accolade on Delaney', *Daily Mail* (London, 21 September 1961) p. 10 [Interview with Behan.]

——, 'Listening in New York to a Gunman Called Behan', *Daily Mail* (London, 25 April 1963) p. 12 [Interview with Behan.]

——, 'Behan: A Giant of a Man, Yet Gentle', *Daily Mail* (London, 21 March 1964) p. 7. [Tribute and recollections.]

——, 'Beneath the Froth', *The New York Times Book Review*, (12 May 1968) p. 10. [Review article and recollections of Behan.]

Alvarez, A., 'The Anti-Establishment Drama', *Partisan Review*, XXVI (Fall 1959) 606–611. [Behan and other dramatists of the late 1950s.]

'American Tributes to Behan', *Evening Herald* (Dublin, 21 March 1964) p. 1. [By *New York Herald Tribune*, Connolly Cole, and James McGill.]

Anderson, Rick, 'Behan's Last', *Sunday Olympian* (Washington, D.C., 28 June 1964) p. 5. [*The Scarperer.*]

Aragno, Riccardo, 'Do-It-Yourself Drama', *Gemini Dialogue*, III (1960) 31–34. [*The Hostage.*]

Archer, Kane, 'Verse and Version', *Books Ireland* (Dublin), No. 11 (March 1977) 49. [Dramatized version of *Borstal Boy*.]

——, 'Pikemen', *Books Ireland* (Dublin), No. 15 (July 1977) 146. [Review article.]

Arnold, Bruce, 'Beckett and Behan and a Theatre in Dublin', *The Dubliner*, II, No. 1 (Spring 1963) 84. [Review article.]

'Art', *Model Housekeeping* (Dublin, November 1954) 7. [On Beatrice Behan, Behan's wife.]

Aspler, Tony, 'Brendan Behan's Last Wake in Montreal', *The Montrealer*, XL (September 1966) 19–20, 35–37. [Recollections of Behan.]

'At the Unveiling of a Bronze Head of Brendan Behan', *Evening Press* (Dublin, 9 June 1975) p. 3. [At 70 Kildare Road, Crumlin, Dublin.]

Atkinson, Brooks, 'Behan Boxes the Conversational Compass; From People to Plays to Bar Mitzvahs', *The New York Times*, (9 December 1960) p. 28: Reprinted in *Tuesdays and Fridays* (New York: Random House, 1963) pp. 19–21 [Interview with Behan.]

'Australia Bans 19 Books', *The Times* (London, 9 January 1959) p. 8. [Including *Borstal Boy*.]

'Australia Lifts Ban on 33 Books', *The New York Times*, (11 August 1963) p. 73. [Including *Borstal Boy*.]

Aynsley, Cyril, 'Man on TV "Had a Few Drinks"', *Daily Express* (London, 19 June 1956) p. 1. [Behan's drunken appearance on BBC TV, interviewed by Malcolm Muggeridge.]

Ayre, Leslie, 'It Looks To Me: Opening the Windows', *Evening News* (London, 19 June 1956) p. 3. [Behan's drunken appearance on BBC TV, interviewed by Malcolm Muggeridge.]

'BBC Reply on Artists' Drinks', *The Daily Telegraph* (London, 23 June 1956) p. 9. [Behan's drunken appearance on BBC TV, interviewed by Malcolm Muggeridge.]

B., C. A., 'Second Half of Behan Life Full of His Peculiarities', *Buffalo News*, (25 June 1966). [*Confessions of an Irish Rebel*.]

B., W., 'Brendan Behan Rambles on New York Sidewalks', *Plain Dealer* (Cleveland, Ohio, 29 November 1964) Section BB, p. 5. [*Brendan Behan's New York*.]

B-R., G. 'Televiews: A Bigger Helping', *The Star* (London, 19 June 1956) p. 6 [Behan's drunken appearance on BBC TV, interviewed by Malcolm Muggeridge.]

Babenko, V. G., 'Problemy tvorčestva irlandskogo pisatelja Brendana Bièna', ['Problems in the Work of the Irish Writer Brendan

Behan'] *Filologičeskie Nauki*, XVIII, No. 1 (1976) 46–54.
'Baby for the Behans', *Daily Express* (London, 31 July 1963) p. 3.
   [Beatrice Behan expecting.]
'Baby Girl for Behans', *The Irish Press* (Dublin, 25 November 1963)
   p. 12. [Blanaid Behan born.]
'Ban on Behan Book Lifted', *The Irish Times* (Dublin, 17 February
   1970) p. 1. [*Borstal Boy*.]
Barkham, John, 'Pub-Crawling in Dublin with Dynamic Mr. Behan',
   The Vancouver Sun, (14 November 1962) p. 5. [*Brendan Behan's Island*.]
——, 'Behan Pens a Valentine', *New York World-Telegram*, (10
   November 1964) p. 63. [*Brendan Behan's New York*.]
Baro, Gene, 'An Exuberant Irishman Adds to the World's Great
   Prison Literature', *New York Herald Tribune Book Review*, (22
   February 1959) p. 5. [*Borstal Boy*.]
Barrett, William, 'Warmth at the Pub', *Atlantic Monthly* (Boston),
   CCXIII (February 1964) 143. [*Hold Your Hour and Have Another*.]
——, 'Places and Pictures', *Atlantic Monthly* (Boston), CCXV (January
   1965) 130. [*Brendan Behan's New York*.]
'Beating the Gargle', *Theatre Arts* (New York), XLVII (February 1963)
   9. [Behan no longer has the stamina to produce a major work.]
Behan, Beatrice, 'What It's Like to Marry a Genius', *Woman's Mirror*
   (London, 7 November 1958) 11. Reprinted as 'My Husband
   Brendan Behan', *The Irish Digest* (Dublin), LXIV, No. 4
   (February 1959) 12–14. [Recollections of Behan.]
——, 'Brendan Behan', *The Observer* (London, 26 July 1970) p. 8.
   [Letter to the Editor defending Behan from charges of
   homosexuality made by his biographer Ulick O'Connor.]
Behan, Brendan, 'The Woman on the Corner of the Next Block to
   Us', *Vogue*, CXXVIII (December 1956) 85, 96. [Autobiographical
   article.]
——, 'Confessions of an Irish Rebel', *The New York Times*, (16
   November 1958) Section 2, p. 3. [Autobiographical article.]
Behan, Brian, 'Brendan', *The Spectator* (London), CCXIII (17 July
   1964) 77–79. Forms chapter 30 in his *With Breast Expanded*
   (London: MacGibbon & Kee, 1964) pp. 200–208. [Evaluation
   and recollections by Brendan's brother.]
Behan, Dominic, 'The Funeral of Brendan Behan', *Life*, International
   Edition, XXXVI, No. 7 (20 April 1964) 32 [Obituary by
   Brendan's brother.]
Behan, Stephen, 'Stephen Behan on Book about Brendan', *Evening
   Herald* (Dublin, 29 November 1965) p. 5. [Letter to the Editor by

Behan's father on Brendan and the Irish Republican Movement.]
    See reply by Anthony Butler, ibid, (1 December 1965) p. 6.
'Behan Again Critical', *The Irish Press* (Dublin, 18 March 1964) p. 1.
'Behan Again Critically Ill', *Evening Press* (Dublin, 18 March 1964) p. 1.
'Behan and Andrews', *Evening Press* (Dublin, 24 April 1964) p. 12.
    [Interview with Behan.]
'Behan Arrested in Toronto', *The New York Times*, (23 March 1961)
    p. 29. [After a fight with a hotel detective and a policeman,
    following an all-night drinking spree.]
'Behan As Others Saw Him', *Evening Press* (Dublin, 21 March 1964)
    p. 9. [Tributes and recollections.]
'Behan Battled, Bailed Out, Bounced', *The Globe and Mail* (Toronto,
    23 March 1961) p. 29. [Remanded in court on charges resulting
    from an overnight spree in Toronto.]
'Behan Benched', *Daily News* (New York, 16 March 1961) p. 43.
    [Behan denied permission to participate in N.Y. St. Patrick's Day
    Parade.]
'Behan Dies', *Daily Mail* (London, 21 March 1964) p. 1.
'Behan Dies in Deep Coma', *The Irish Times* (Dublin, 21 March 1964)
    p. 1.
'Behan Disappears into Limbo', *The New York Times*, (30 July 1961)
    p. 47. [Leaves Jersey City Medical Center.]
'Behan Enters Alcoholics Clinic for Treatment', *The Globe and Mail*
    (Toronto, 28 March 1961) p. 12. [Sunnyside Private Hospital,
    Toronto.]
'Behan Faces Jail Term', *The New York Times*, (2 June 1961) p. 37.
    [On a charge of disturbing the peace, as a result of getting drunk
    in Hollywood.]
'Behan Gave Up Book Rights', *The Irish Press* (Dublin, 10 November
    1962) p. 7. [*Brendan Behan's Island.*]
'Behan Gets into Act at London Theatre', *The New York Times*, (10
    July 1959) p. 28. [At Wyndham's Theatre, where *The Hostage* was
    being staged.]
'Behan Gravely Ill in the Meath Hospital', *The Irish Times* (Dublin, 16
    March 1964) p. 1.
'Behan Guilty, Fined $200', *The Toronto Daily Star*, (27 April 1961)
    p. 1. [On two charges of assault and one of creating a disturbance
    in Toronto.]
'Behan Here, Might "Join the Fire Dept" ', *Boston Evening American*, (2
    September 1960) p. 5. [Interview with Behan.]
'Behan Improves Slightly; Gardai Uncertain What Caused Injuries',

The Irish Times (Dublin, 31 December 1963) p. 1. [Behan found unconscious on roadway.]

'Behan in Coma', *The Daily Telegraph* (London), (18 March 1964) p. 1.

'Behan in Jersey City', *The New York Times*, (18 March 1961) p. 46. [As the St. Patrick's Day guest of the city after being banned from the New York parade.]

'Behan Injury Caused by Fall', *The New York Times*, (1 January 1964) p. 16. [In hospital in Dublin.]

'Behan Is Fined $200', *The New York Times*, (28 April 1961) p. 25. [After having been convicted on two charges of assault and one of creating disturbance in Toronto.]

'Behan Is Slightly Improved', *Evening Press* (Dublin, 16 March 1964) p. 1; and (17 March 1964) p. 1.

'Behan Leaves Hospital', *The New York Times*, (13 January 1964) p. 24. [After fall on road near Dublin.]

'Behan Loses His Place in St. Patrick's Parade', *The New York Times*, (14 March 1961) p. 71. [As an honorary member of the Gaelic Society of Fordham University.]

'Behan Misses the Boat', *The New York Times*, (29 July 1961) p. 8. [And winds up instead in the Jersey City Medical Center.]

'Behan Not Allowed Visitors', *Evening Herald* (Dublin, 31 December 1963) p. 7. [Behan in hospital recovering from head injuries after being found lying on roadway.]

'Behan – O Beachain', *Der Spiegel*, XVIII, No. 24 (1963) 78–80. [*Borstal Boy*.]

'Behan of the Press', *Newsweek* (New York), LXIII (3 February 1964) 82–83. [*Hold Your Hour and Have Another*.]

'Behan Seriously Ill in Hospital', *The New York Times*, (31 March 1960) p. 29. [In London.]

'Behan Sinks into Coma', *The Irish Press* (London, 19 March 1964) p. 1. [In Dublin.]

'Behan – "Slow Progress"', *The Irish Press* (Dublin, 17 March 1964) p. 1. [In Dublin.]

'Behan, Stage Irishman in Real Life', *The Daily Telegraph* (London, 21 March 1964) p. 14. [Obituary.]

'Behan Still Critical', *The Irish Press* (Dublin, 20 March 1964) p. 1. [In Dublin.]

'Behan Still Gravely Ill', *The Irish Times* (Dublin, 17 March 1964) p. 1. [In Dublin.]

'Behan . . . the Turbulent Genius', *Evening Herald* (Dublin, 21 March

1964) p. 3. [Tributes to Behan.]

'Behan the Wild One Dies in Hospital', *Belfast Telegraph*, (21 March 1964) p. 2. [In Dublin.]

'Behan To Be Buried Today in Dublin', *The Irish Times* (Dublin, 23 March 1964) p. 1.

'Behan Was Not Hit by Car', *Evening Press* (Dublin, 31 December 1963) p. 1. [Behan found unconscious on roadway in Dublin.]

'Behan's Account of New York Told with Wit', *Catholic Standard* (Washington, D.C., 20 November 1964). [*Brendan Behan's New York.*]

'Behan's Binge Lands Him in Toronto Jail, Bail $500', *The Toronto Daily Star*, (22 March 1961) pp. 1, 8. [Behan charged with assault and causing a disturbance.]

'Behan's Condition Unchanged', *The Irish Times* (Dublin, 20 March 1964) p. 1. [Behan seriously ill in Dublin.]

'Behan's Last Play Complete as Wife Uncovers 20 Pages', *The New York Times*, (28 December 1971) p. 25. [*Richard's Cork Leg.*]

'Behan's Soul Was Full of Poetry', *Evening Press* (Dublin, 21 March 1964) p. 9. [Swedish tributes.]

'Behan's Widow Alters Home to Get Income from Rents', *The New York Times*, (3 February 1965) p. 29.

Belser, Lee, 'Life Never Boring for Wife of Behan', *Los Angeles Mirror* (29 May 1961) p. 2. [Interview with Beatrice Behan.]

Bergamo, Ralph, 'Behan's Savory Irish Stew', *Atlanta Journal Constitution*, (15 May 1966). [*Confessions of an Irish Rebel.*]

Bess, Donovan, 'China Plate Rhymes with Mate', *San Francisco Chronicle*, (8 March 1959) p. 16. [*Borstal Boy.*]

Bestic, Alan, 'Meet the New Brendan Behan', *The Irish Digest* (Dublin), LXIX, No. 4 (October 1960) 13–16. [Recollections of Behan.]

——, 'Broke – But He Gave a Coin to My Child', *Today* (London, 25 April 1964) 24–25. [Recollections of Behan.]

Binzen, Peter H., 'Teacups Tinkle for Author: Irish Playwright Behan Switches to Tea in Visit Here', *The Evening Bulletin* (Philadelphia, 12 November 1960) p. 3. [Interview with Behan.]

'Birthday Remand for Brendan Behan; Charged with Assault on Police', *The Times* (London, 10 February 1961) p. 5. [In Dublin.]

Black, Peter, 'Teleview', *The Daily Mail* (London, 19 June 1956) p. 12. [Behan's drunken appearance on BBC TV, interviewed by Malcolm Muggeridge.]

'Black Monday on BBC TV', *Sunderland Echo* (Sunderland, 21 June

1956) p. 4. [Behan's drunken appearance on BBC TV,
interviewed by Malcolm Muggeridge.]

Blackburn, Bob, 'Midnight Zone Gets a Reprieve: Brendan Behan',
Toronto Daily Star, (22 March 1961) p. 18. [Behan on CFTO
'Better Late' programme in Toronto.]

'Blanking Success', *Time* (Chicago), LXXII (8 December 1958) 78–
80. [Interview with Behan.]

Blau, Herbert, 'Littlewood and Planchon in an Affluent Society',
Encore (London), VII, No. 2 (March–April 1960) 7–14. [Joan
Littlewood's production of *The Hostage*, passim.]

Block, George, 'Some Irish Words about New York', *Tulsa World*, (6
December 1964). [*Brendan Behan's New York.*]

Blythe, Ernest, 'Tribute', *The Irish Times* (Dublin, 21 March 1964) p. 1.

Bold, Alan, 'It Depends on the Liver', *Tribune* (London, 23 December
1966) p. 17. [Review article.]

Boorne, Bill, 'Show News: Off My Cuff', *Evening News* (London, 2
June 1956) p. 6. [Offers for filming of *The Quare Fellow* by four
companies.]

'Borstal Boy', *Die Kiepe* (Köln, April 1963) p. 2. [*Borstal Boy.*]

'*Borstal Boy* by Brendan Behan', *The Listener* (London), LX (6
November 1958) 743.

'The Borstal Boy Legend', *The Times Literary Supplement* (London, 31
July 1970) p. 850. [Review article.]

'Bottle Honours', *The Times Literary Supplement* (London, 8 March
1974) p. 230. [Review article.]

Bouchart, D., 'Brendan Behan en Liberté dans les pubs de Dublin',
Arts (Paris, 8–14 April 1959) p. 4. [Biographical study.]

Boylan, Clare, 'Behan's Mother Wasn't There', *Evening Press* (Dublin,
11 October 1967) p. 3. [Interview with Kathleen Behan, Behan's
mother.]

Boyle, Patrick, 'The Writer as Barfly', *Book World* (*Chicago Tribune*), (6
June 1971) 16–19. [Review article.]

Bradley, Van Allen, 'Behan on Dublin Pubs', *Long Island Press*, (25
November 1962) Section 7 p. 9. [*Brendan Behan's Island.*]

Bradshaw, Bob, 'Early Behan', *The Irish Times* (Dublin, 9 July 1970)
p. 12. [Recollections of Behan.]

Brady, Seamus, 'The Behan They Don't Know', *Daily Express*
(London, 12 June 1963) p. 5. [Recollections of Behan.]

——, 'The Love Match of Brendan and Beatrice', *The Irish Digest*
(Dublin), LXXVIII, No. 2 (August 1963) 75–78. [Interview with
Behan.]

——, 'We Shall Never See His Like Again', *Daily Express* (London, 24 March 1964) p. 5. [Behan mourned in Dublin.]

Braine, John, 'Irishman in the Limelight', *The Sunday Telegraph* (London, 30 October 1966) p. 16. [Review article.]

Braithwaite, Dennis, 'A Curse on Canada, Behan Says', *The Globe and Mail* (Toronto, 10 April 1961) p. 11. [Interview with Behan.]

Breatnach, Deasún, 'Breandán Ó Beacháin', *The United Irishman* (Dublin), XVI (May 1964) 5. [Tribute to Behan.]

'Brendan Behan', *The Daily Telegraph* (London, 13 July 1959) p. 7. [Behan's wife Beatrice Behan tells of Brendan's treatment for diabetes.]

'Brendan Behan', *Current Biography* (New York), XXII, No. 3 (March 1961) 7–9. [Biographical note.]

'Brendan Behan', *Dublin Evening Mail*, (5 April 1961) p. 5. [In hospital in Toronto.]

'Brendan Behan', *Evening Press* (Dublin, 19 March 1964) p. 1. [Critically ill in Dublin.]

'Brendan Behan', *Publishers' Weekly* (Philadelphia), CLXXXV (30 March 1964) 37. [Obituary.]

'Brendan Behan', *New York Journal American*, (21 March 1964) p. 10. [Editorial tribute.]

'Brendan Behan Again', *The Rocky Mount Telegram* (North Carolina), (4 September 1966) p. 12. [*Confessions of an Irish Rebel*.]

'Brendan Behan Again in Coma', *The Irish Times* (Dublin, 19 March 1964) p. 1. [In Dublin.]

'Brendan Behan – Alas! Not at His Best', *Sunday Star* (Washington, D.C., 21 April 1964) p. C5. [*The Scarperer*.]

'Brendan Behan: An Appreciation', *The United Irishman* (Dublin), XVI (April 1964), 2.

'Brendan Behan Dies at 41', *The Daily Telegraph* (London, 21 March 1964) p. 1. [In Dublin.]

'Brendan Behan Dies in Coma', *Belfast News-Letter*, (21 March 1964) p. 1.

'Brendan Behan Dies in Coma', *The Cork Examiner*, (21 March 1964) pp. 1, 20.

'Brendan Behan Dies in Dublin', *The New York Times*, (21 March 1964) p. 25. [Obituary.]

'Brendan Behan Dies With Wife at Bedside', *Daily Express* (London, 21 March 1964) p. 1.

'Brendan Behan Fined £2', *Evening Herald* (Dublin, 6 March 1959) p. 1. [For being drunk and disorderly near Dublin.]

'Brendan Behan Fined £2 at Bray', *Irish Independent* (Dublin, 7 March

1959) p. 12. [For being drunk and disorderly.]

'Brendan Behan Fined 40s. for being Disorderly', *Evening Press* (Dublin, 6 March 1959) pp. 1, 6. [At Bray, near Dublin.]

'Brendan Behan Fined £30', *The Times* (London, 18 February 1961) p. 4. [For assault in Dublin.]

'Brendan Behan Fined £30 on Assault Charges', *The Irish Times* (Dublin, 18 February 1961) p. 5. [Detailed report on the trial.]

'Brendan Behan Has Small Operation', *Evening Press* (Dublin, 20 March 1964) p. 1. [In Meath Hospital, Dublin, but still in a continual coma.]

'Brendan Behan Hospitalized', *The New York Times*, (29 March 1961) p. 35. [Described as 'a very sick man' in Toronto.]

'Brendan Behan Hospitalized', *The New York Times*, (20 August 1963) p. 38. [In Dublin.]

'Brendan Behan Hurt in Road Near Dublin', *The New York Times*, (30 December 1963) p. 3. [In hospital for injuries.]

'Brendan Behan Injured', *Irish Independent* (Dublin, 30 December 1963) p. 1. [Behan admitted to Meath Hospital after being found unconscious on roadway.]

'Brendan Behan Insists on Use of Irish in Bray Court', *The Irish Times* (Dublin, 7 March 1959) p. 9. [Behan fined 40s. for being drunk and disorderly near Dublin.]

'Brendan Behan Is Dead', *Daily Worker* (London, 21 March 1964) p. 1.

'Brendan Behan Is Dead', *The Irish Press* (Dublin, 21 March 1964) p. 1.

'Brendan Behan Is In Coma', *The New York Times*, (16 March 1964) p. 36. [In Dublin hospital.]

'Brendan Behan: Man and Showman', *The Times* (London, 7 September 1968) p. 20. [Brief review article.]

'Brendan Behan: Man of Compassion', *The Guardian* (London, 21 March 1964) p. 3. [Obituary.]

'Brendan Behan, Noted Writer, Dies in Dublin', *Irish Independent* (Dublin, 21 March 1964) p. 14. [Obituary.]

'Brendan Behan on Television Tonight', *The Irish Times* (Dublin, 21 July 1956) p. 1. [On the British Independent Television programme 'Show Talk'.]

'Brendan Behan – the End', *Daily Herald* (London, 21 March 1964) p. 1. [Behan dies in Dublin.]

'Brendan Behan – "Very Grave" ', *The Irish Times* (Dublin, 18 March 1964) p. 1. [In Dublin hospital.]

'Brendan Behan: "Very Grave" ', *Irish Independent* (Dublin, 19 March 1964) p. 1. [In Dublin hospital.]

'Brendan Behan Visits Hub', *Boston American*, (2 September 1960). [Interview with Behan.]

'Brendan Behan's Father, 79', *The New York Times*, (14 July 1967) p. 31. [Dies.]

'Brendan Behan's New York', *Clearwater Sun*, (8 November 1964) p. 8-D. [*Brendan Behan's New York*.]

'Brendan Behan's Raucous Memoir', *Lake Charles American Press*, (16 July 1966) p. 6. [*Confessions of an Irish Rebel*.]

'Brendan Behan's Widow', *The Irish Times* (Dublin, 8 March 1974) p. 1. [Beatrice Behan unveils a plaque honouring 14 Russell Street, Dublin, where Behan was reared.]

'Brendan Hits the Bottle', *Dublin Daily Chronicle*, I, No. 3 (28 October 1960) 1. [Behan back on the booze in New York after 12 months 'on the dry'.]

'Brendan in Colour', *Sunday Independent* (Dublin, 13 September 1970) p. 19. [Film on Behan to be shown on BBC TV programme 'Omnibus'.]

'Brendan Intensely Religious', *Evening Press* (Dublin, 30 March 1964) p. 3. [Recollections of Behan by C. A. Joyce, the former Governor of Hollesley Bay Borstal Institution.]

'Brendan Is Weaker', *Evening Press* (Dublin, 20 March 1964) p. 1. [In Dublin hospital.]

'Brendan Sees Toronto's Bars', *The Telegram* (Toronto, 22 March 1961) p. 1. [Behan charged with assault and causing a disturbance.]

'Brendan the Novelist', *Evening Herald* (Dublin, 25 November 1966) p. 14. [*The Scarperer*.]

'Brendan Tries a Bit of Irish', *Daily Mail* (London, 7 March 1959) p. 3. [Behan fined for disorderly behaviour at Bray, near Dublin.]

'Brendan, We Hardly Knew You', *Sunday World* (Dublin, 10 July 1977) p. 22 [Review article.]

Breslin, Jimmy, 'Himself, Tossed Off in Short Snorts', *New York Herald Tribune*, (2 February 1964) pp. 5, 21. [*Hold Your Hour and Have Another*.]

Brien, Alan, 'Tribute', *Evening Press* (Dublin, 21 March 1964) p. 9.

——, 'Brendan Behan: "Uproarious Tragedy"', *The Sunday Telegraph* (London, 22 March 1964) p. 19. [Recollections of Behan.]

——, 'New View of Brendan Behan', *The New York Times*, (31 August 1970) p. 23. [Review article.]

Brockman, Zoe, 'Novels by the Behan Brothers Give Readers a Pretty

Heady Dose of Life', *Gastonia Gazette* (North Carolina, 31 July
1966). [*Confessions of an Irish Rebel*.]

Brown, Christy, 'Brendan', *The Holy Door* (Dublin), No. 1 (Summer
1965) 3–4. [A poem.]

Brydon, Arthur, 'Behan Brings Back New Hate – Publishers', *The Globe
and Mail* (Toronto, 20 March 1961) p. 17. [Interview with Behan.]

Buchloh, Paul G., 'Brendan Behans *The Hostage*: Lachende Hinnahme
einer bitteren und chaotischen Welt', *Literatur in Wissenschaft und
Unterricht* (Kiel), IV (1971) 215–236.

Buchwald, Art, 'Ireland's Enfant Terrible', *New York Herald Tribune*,
(23 March 1959) International ed., p. 5. [Interview with Behan.]

Burgess, Anthony, 'The Writer As Drunk', *The Spectator* (London),
CCXVII (4 November 1966) 588. Reprinted in *Urgent Copy*
(London: Jonathan Cape; New York: W. W. Norton, 1968) pp.
88–92. [Review article.]

'The Burying of Brendan', *Evening Press* (Dublin, 23 March 1964) pp.
1, 4.

'Busy, Busy Days for Beatrice', *Evening Press* (Dublin, 29 April 1964)
p. 5. [Newly-widowed Beatrice Behan trying to settle Behan's
affairs.]

Butler, Anthony, 'Brendan Behan', *Evening Herald* (Dublin, 1
December 1965) p. 6. [Behan and the Irish Republican
Movement.]

——, 'The Last of the Dubliners', *Evening Herald* (Dublin, 3 June
1977) p. 8. [Review article.]

Byrne, Frank, 'The Forgotten Grave of Brendan Behan', *Sunday
Independent* (Dublin, 12 June 1977) p. 7. [Though Behan is buried
in Glasnevin, the Irish national cemetery, his grave is still
unmarked.]

——, 'Irish Group Plan for a Memorial', *Sunday Independent* (Dublin, 8
January 1978) p. 9. [A headstone for Behan is planned at last.]

C., M., 'The World of Brendan Behan', *The Irish Times* (Dublin, 13
November 1965) p. 8. [Review article.]

C., N., 'Carman's the Pulse in "Impulse"', *The Toronto Daily Star*, (18
March 1961) p. 27. [Behan as conferencier in the revue 'Impulse'
at the O'Keefe Centre, Toronto.]

Cail, Harold L. 'Playwright's Island', *Portland Evening Express* (Maine,
28 November 1962) p. 16. [*Brendan Behan's Island*.]

Callery, Sean, 'Brendan Behan: The Ignominy of Success', *The
Commonweal* (New York), XCIII (23 October 1970) 87–91.
[Recollections of Behan.]

Calta, Louis. 'Behan Comments on the Theatre; Irish Dramatist Arrives for Opening of Play–Backs Critics and Kennedy', *The New York Times*, (3 September 1960) p. 8. [Interview with Behan.]

——, 'Version of Play by Behan to Bow', *The New York Times*, (23 September 1973) p. 62. [*Richard's Cork Leg*.]

Campbell, Michael, 'Book and Author', *The Irish Times* (Dublin), (25 October 1958) p. 6. [Recollections of Behan.]

——, 'Streets Broad and Narrow', *Saturday Review* (New York), XLV (3 November 1962) 48. [*Brendan Behan's Island*.]

Capouya, Emile, 'The Gift of Gab on the Lam', *Saturday Review* (New York), XLVII (20 June 1964) 36–37. [*The Scarperer*.]

Carty, Francis, 'Behan: Triumph and Tragedy of a Great Talent', *The Sunday Press* (Dublin, 26 July 1970) p. 17. [Review article.]

Caulfield, Max, 'A Portrait of Brendan Behan Drinking Life's Last Bitter Dregs', *Fact* (New York), III (January–February 1966) 18–25. [Recollections of Behan.]

Cavan, Romilly, 'Scripts', *Plays and Players* (London), XXI (November 1973) 71. [*Richard's Cork Leg*.]

'Censorship Board Bans 23 Books', *The Irish Times* (Dublin, 12 November 1958) p. 7. [Including *Borstal Boy*.]

Chase, Mary, 'Irish Wit Views New York Personalities', *Rocky Mountain News* (Denver, Colorado, 8 November 1964) p. 20. [*Brendan Behan's New York*.]

Chichester, 'No Drink for Sash-Singing Brendan', *Belfast Telegraph*, (28 August 1962) p. 3. [Behan refused drink in a Dublin bar.]

'Child to Brendan Behan', *The New York Times*, (27 November 1963) p. 31. [Blanaid Behan.]

Childers, Roderick W., 'Brendan Behan', *Chicago Today*, III (1966) 50–54. [Recollections of Behan.]

——, 'In Uneven Playbacks, the Life of Rebellious Brendan Behan', *National Observer* (New York), V (6 June 1966) 21. [*Confessions of an Irish Rebel*.]

'City's Final Salute to "Rebel" Son', *Evening Herald* (Dublin, 23 March 1964) p. 1. [Behan's funeral.]

'Classics Eclipsed', *Plays and Players* (London), VI, No. 11 (August 1959) 20. [The book version of *The Hostage*.]

Cohen, Nathan, 'Incoherent "Impulse!"' *The Toronto Daily Star*, (21 March 1961) p. 18. [Behan as conferencier in the revue 'Impulse' at the O'Keefe Centre, Toronto.]

Cole, Connolly, 'The Gusto That Was Behan', *Chicago Daily News*, (27 June 1964) p. 8. [*The Scarperer*.]

——, 'Confessions of an Irish Rebel', The Dublin Magazine, V (Spring 1966) 95.

Cole, Joseph, 'Brendan', Books and Bookmen (London), XIII (November 1967) 34–35. Reprinted as 'Brendan, I Hardly Know You!' Quadrant; An Australian Bi-Monthly, LIX (1969) 46–50. [Recollections of Behan.]

——, 'Night Out in Dublin', Meanjin Quarterly, XXVII (September 1968) 309–321. Reprinted in The Dublin Magazine, VIII (Spring–Summer 1969) 5–18. [Recollections of Behan.]

Connolly, Cyril, 'Behan & Borstal Share the Credit', The Sunday Times (London, 19 October 1958) p. 17. [Borstal Boy.]

——, 'Pub-Crawls and Golf-Clubs', The Sunday Times (London, 30 September 1962) p. 32. [Brendan Behan's Island.]

Coogan, Tim Pat, 'In Defence of Brendan Behan', The Irish Digest (Dublin), LXXII, No. 1 (July 1961) 15–18. [Recollections of Behan.]

——, 'The Man Brendan Behan', Evening Press (Dublin, 21 March 1964) p. 9. [Tribute to and recollections of Behan.]

——, 'Closing Time', The Spectator (London), CCXII (27 March 1964) 406. [Obituary.]

Cook, Bruce, 'Brendan Behan: A Last Look', Catholic Magazine, (December 1964) 27–32. [Tribute to Behan.]

Cooley, Franklin D., 'New York As Viewed by Behan', Richmond Times-Dispatch (Virginia, 22 November 1964) p. L-11. [Brendan Behan's New York.]

Corbett, James 'Theatre Workshop: A British People's Theatre', Meanjin (Melbourne), XVIII (September 1959) 327–333. [The Quare Fellow and The Hostage, passim.]

Corke, Hilary, 'Nannie to Novels', The Listener (London), LXXVI (1 December 1966) 819. [The Scarperer.]

Costella, Carl, 'Ire of Ireland: Brendan Behan Was Rebel with a Heart', Duluth News Tribune (Minnesota, 5 June 1966) Cosmopolitan Section p. 2. [Confessions of an Irish Rebel.]

Coughlan, Anthony, 'With Brendan Behan to Traynor's Funeral', The Irish Democrat (London), No. 229 (January 1964) pp. 6, 9. [Interview with Behan.]

Coughley, Sherry Kafka, 'Behan Book from Tapes Has Vitality', Morning Star-Telegram (Fort Worth, Texas, 26 June 1966). [Confessions of an Irish Rebel.]

Court, Monty, 'Behan Comes Back a Far, Far Quieter Fellow, But Still Talking', Daily Mail (London, 15 October 1959) p. 7.

[Interview with Behan.]

Cromie, Robert, 'Brendan Behan Gives Views of New York', *Chicago Tribune*, (16 November 1964) Section 2, p. 2. [*Brendan Behan's New York.*]

Cronin, Sean, 'Where the Martyrs Died', *The Nation* (New York), CCIII (7 November 1966) 486–488. [*Confessions of an Irish Rebel.*]

——, 'Bagot Street Bard', *Commonweal* (New York, 12 January 1968), 447–448. [Patrick Kavanagh 'Made a Steadfast stand against what he called "Behanism" '.]

——, 'Sting-a-Ling-a-Ling', *The Nation* (New York), CCVI (13 May 1968) 642–644. [Review article.]

'Crowds Mourn Brendan Behan', *The Age* (Melbourne, 24 March 1964) p. 4.

Curley, Thomas F., 'Behan's Book', *The Commonweal* (New York), LXIX (13 March 1959) 628–629. [*Borstal Boy.*]

Curtiss, Thomas Quinn, 'Irish Author, Playwright – and Talker', *New York Herald Tribune Book Review*, (25 February 1962) p. 8. [Interview with Behan.]

Daly, Cormac, O. F. M., 'Priest's Tribute', *The Sunday Press* (Dublin, 22 March 1964) p. 6. [Obituary.]

Damisch, Isabel M., 'Theatre Workshop: A British People's Theatre', *Recherches Anglaises et Américaines*, V (1972) 121–140. [Includes discussions of *The Quare Fellow* and *The Hostage.*]

Davies, Stan, 'Shed a Tear for Brendan', *Saturday Night* (Toronto), LXXIX (May 1964) 16–18. [Recollections of Behan.]

'Death and the Irish', *The Times Literary Supplement*, (26 April 1974) p. 440 [*Richard's Cork Leg.*]

'Death of Brendan Behan', *The Guardian* (London, 21 March 1964) p. 1.

'Death of Brendan Behan', *Irish Independent* (Dublin, 21 March 1964) p. 1.

'Debater'. 'Brendan as a Debater', *Evening Press* (Dublin, 2 April 1964) p. 11. [Letter to the Editor.]

DeBurca,.Seamus, 'Profile of Brendan Behan: The Quare Fellow', *The Irish Digest* (Dublin), LVII, No. 4 (October 1956) 13–14. [Biographical sketch by Behan's cousin.]

——, 'In Search of Stephen Behan', *The Irish Digest* (Dublin), LXXVII, No. 9 (March 1963) 43–46. [Recollections of Behan's parents.]

——, 'The Background of Brendan Behan', *Waterfront* (Dublin), III, No. 7 (August 1963) 10–11. [Recollections of Behan.]

——,'The Essential Brendan Behan', *Modern Drama*, VIII, No. 4 (Spring 1966) 374–381. [Recollections of Behan.]

Delargy, Hugh 'Broth of a Boy', *Tribune* (London, 24 October 1958) p. 10. [*Borstal Boy.*]

——, 'Behan', *Sunday Citizen* (22 March 1964) p. 6. [Recollections of Behan.]

Delehanty, James, 'The Quarter: A Look Back; Six Hours with Brendan', *The Kilkenny Magazine*, No. 2 (Autumn 1960) 41–44. [Interview with Behan.]

'Denies She Said Behan Left Fortune', *Evening Press* (Dublin, 8 June 1964) p. 1. [Rae Jeffs, who looked after Behan's English financial affairs, denies a report in which she was quoted as saying that Behan's assets would be in excess of £70,000.]

Dennis, Nigel, 'Behind the Blarney', *The Sunday Telegraph* (London, 30 September 1962) p. 6. [*Brendan Behan's Island.*]

'Discussion on Irish Theatre Misfired', *The Irish Times* (Dublin), (27 February 1961) p. 5. [Report on discussion by panel comprising Brendan Behan, John B. Keane, Ray MacAnally, and Seamus Kelly.]

'The Doctors Warn Behan', *Daily Mail* (London, 12 June 1959) p. 3. [Interview with Behan.]

Donnelly, Peter, 'Behan: A Minor Writer but Built to Last', *Irish Independent* (Dublin, 4 July 1977) p. 8. [Review article.]

' "Don't Like This Dying Lark at All" ', *The Irish Times* (Dublin, 21 March 1964) p. 9. [Recollections of Behan by two former teachers.]

Dorn, Norman K., 'Among the New Books', *San Francisco Chronicle*, (25 August 1957) p. 23. [*The Quare Fellow.*]

Doyle, Edward, '*The Scarperer*', *Book-of-the-Month-Club News*, (August 1964).

Drabble, Margaret, 'An Echo of Behan', *The Sunday Times* (London, 31 October 1965), p. 52. [*Confessions of an Irish Rebel.*]

'Dublin Boy Goes to Borstal; "Sent to Organise Explosives" ', *The Irish Times* (Dublin, 8 February 1940) p. 6. [Behan sentenced to three years' Borstal detention on IRA activities in Liverpool.]

'Dublin Gives Behan a Hero's Funeral', *The New York Times*, (24 March 1964) p. 35.

'Dublin Stops for Brendan Behan', *The Sunday Express* (London, 22 March 1964) p. 17. [Behan's funeral.]

Dunkley, Chris, 'Omnibus: Brendan Behan', *The Times* (London, 5 April 1971) p. 8. [BBC TV programme on Behan.]

Duprey, Richard A., 'The Bloodshot World of Brendan Behan', *The Critic* (Chicago), XX (Dec 1961–Jan 1962) 55–57. ['The most disturbing thing . . . is that much of what he says is true'.]

Dyroff, Jan M., 'Pulling the Id from Idiosyncrasy', *Patriot Ledger* (Quincy, Mass., 10 August 1966) p. 36. [*Confessions of an Irish Rebel.*]

E., L., 'Behan Found New York an Enchanting Place', *Durham Morning Herald* (15 November 1964) p. 5D. [*Brendan Behan's New York.*]

Edwards, John D., 'Brendan Behan: rebelle malgré lui', *Les Langues Modernes*, LXI (March 1967) 207–211. [Assessment.]

Edwards, Owen Dudley, 'Behan at Play', *Tribune* (London, 5 October 1962) p. 10. [*Brendan Behan's Island.*]

——, 'Myself When Young', *Tribune* (London, 25 October 1963) p. 9. [*Hold Your Hour and Have Another.*]

Ellison, Bob, 'Brendan Behan', *Rogue* (Evanston, Illinois), VI (May 1961) 51–52, 66. [Interview with Behan.]

Ellmann, Richard, 'A Raucous, Witty Tour of Ireland', *Chicago Sunday Tribune Magazine of Books*, (4 November 1962) p. 2. [*Brendan Behan's Island.*]

Elmes, Judith, 'Ten Years After His Death', *Sunday World* (Dublin), (10 February 1974) p. 10. [Interview with Beatrice Behan.]

'End to Confusion', *Newsweek*, LXIII (30 March 1964) 72 [Obituary.]

Eriksson, Lars-Göran, 'Brendan Behans universitet', *Horisont* (Finland), XVIII, Nos. 3–4 (1971) 56–64. [The world of Brendan Behan.]

Esslin, Martin, 'Brecht and the English Theatre', *Tulane Drama Review*, XI, No. 2 (Winter 1966) 63–70. [*The Hostage*, passim.]

Evans, Ronald, 'Impulse!: A Batter of Bands & Behan', *The Telegram* (Toronto, 21 March 1961) p. 32. [Behan participates in improvisation show 'Impulse!' at the O'Keefe Centre, Toronto.]

——, 'A Trying Tryout for Impulse!' *The Telegram* (Toronto, 23 March 1961) p. 44. [Behan is out of the improvisation show 'Impulse!'.]

Fallon, Gabriel, 'Brendan's Genius', *Evening Press* (Dublin, 27 March 1964) p. 9. [Tribute to and recollections of Behan.]

——, 'Compassion', *The Irish Press* (Dublin, 2 March 1974) p. 8. [Review article.]

Farragher, Bernard, 'Brendan Behan's Unarranged Realism', *Drama Critique*, IV (February 1961) 38–39. [*The Hostage* reveals Behan's debt to O'Casey.]

Farren, Ronan, 'Early Behan', *Irish Independent* (Dublin, 19 November 1966) p. 10. [*The Scarperer.*]

Faulkner, Joe P., 'Behan "The Milkman" Here for a Dry Run', *New York Journal American*, (2 September 1960) p. 3. [Interview with Behan.]

——, 'Winner Goes Shopping for Her Trip to Ireland', *New York Journal-American*, (13 November 1960) p. 30. [Behan as one of three judges who examined contest letters.]

Fay, Gerard, 'Mr. Behan's Public School', *The Manchester Guardian*, (21 October 1958) p. 4. [*Borstal Boy.*]

——, 'Believe Me If All Those . . .', *The Spectator* (London, 5 October 1962) 528. [*Brendan Behan's Island.*]

Fay, Stephen, 'Behan the Excommunicate', *The Sunday Times* (London, 13 November 1966) p. 28. [*The Scarperer.*]

Federman, Raymond, 'Becket and Behan', *Modern Drama*, VIII, No. 1 (May 1965) 123–124. [Review article.]

'Feicreanach', 'In Defence of Brendan Behan', *The Irish Democrat* (London), No. 233 (May 1964) 4–5. [From the treatment of the English press.]

'Fight to Save Life of Playwright', *Irish Independent* (Dublin, 17 March 1964) p. 1.

Finch, Archer, '*Brendan Behan's Island*', *Book-of-the-Month-Club News* (January 1963).

F[inegan], J. J., 'His Place in Drama', *Evening Herald* (Dublin, 21 March 1964) p. 3. [Evaluation.]

——, 'In Iceland, Too, Brendan Was Remembered', *Evening Herald* (Dublin, 4 April 1964) p. 8. [Tribute to Behan.]

——, 'Brendan's Last Comedy in Print', *Evening Herald* (Dublin, 3 November 1973) p. 11. [*Richard's Cork Leg.*]

——, 'Could Brendan's Life Have Been Saved?', *Evening Herald* (Dublin, 19 February 1974) p. 15. [Review article.]

Fisher, Desmond, 'Britain Today: Brendan Behan', *The Irish Press* (Dublin, 21 June 1956) p. 6. [Behan's popularity in London.]

Fitzgerald, Marion, 'Talking to Mrs. Stephen Behan', *The Irish Times* (Dublin, 8 December 1962) p. 10. [Interview with Kathleen Behan, Behan's mother.]

——, 'Mrs. Brendan Behan', *Hibernia* (Dublin), XXVII (January 1963) 9, 11. [Interview with Beatrice Behan, Behan's wife.]

Fitzgerald, Maurice, 'Half an Evening with Behan', *Canadian Forum*, XXXIX (October 1959) 147–148. [Recollections of Behan.]

Fitzpatrick, Rita, 'Behan's Island: Primarily People', *Chicago Sunday*

Times, (16 November 1962). [*Brendan Behan's Island.*]

Fitz-Simon, Christopher, 'The Theater in Dublin', *Modern Drama*, II, No. 3 (December 1959) 289–294. [*The Quare Fellow.*]

Flanagan, Marie, ' "He's Aerach" – Behan's Wife', *The Toronto Daily Star*, (21 March 1961) p. 42. [Interview with Beatrice Behan, Behan's wife.]

Flynn, Arthur, 'A Tribute to Brendan', *Evening Herald* (Dublin), (4 April 1964) p. 4. [Letter to the Editor.]

Foley, Donal, 'Surface Behan', *The Irish Times* (Dublin, 25 July 1970) p. 8. [Review article.]

——, 'Fleet Street Memories', *The Irish Times* (Dublin), (25 January 1978) p. 8. Extracted from *Three Villages: An Autobiography* (Dublin: Egotist Press, 1977) pp. 79–80. [Recollections of Behan.]

'14-Pint Behan Switches to Milk; Man, It's Desperate', *Daily Mail* (London, 3 August 1956) p. 3. [Interview with Behan.]

Fowke, Edith, '*Borstal Boy*', *Canadian Forum*, XXXIX (May 1959) 44.

Freeman, Donald, 'Brendan Behan on a Dry Day', *The San Diego Union*, (2 December 1960) p. A26. [Interview with Behan.]

——, 'Last Legacy of Brendan's Gallic Brew', *The San Diego Union*, (3 July 1966) p. E6. [*Confessions of an Irish Rebel.*]

Friedrich, Otto, 'A Chronicle of Small Beer', *The Reporter* (New York), XX (19 March 1959) 45–46. [*Borstal Boy.*]

'Funeral of Mr. Brendan Behan', *Irish Independent* (Dublin), (24 March 1964) p. 11.

Furlong, Rory, 'New Book on Brendan Behan', *Irish Independent* (Dublin, 29 July 1970) p. 8. [Letter to the Editor by Behan's stepbrother defending Behan from charges of homosexuality made by his biographer Ulick O'Connor.]

Gallagher, F. J., '*My Brother Brendan*', *America* (New York), CXIV (7 May 1966) 668. [Review article.]

Gartner, Carl, 'He Lived While He Lived', *Des Moines Sunday Register*, (1 November 1964) p. 7F. [*Brendan Behan's New York.*]

Gavaghan, Paul, '*Hold Your Hour and Have Another*', *America* (New York), CX (22 February 1964) 261–262.

'Gay Irish Insults', *Life*, XLIX (19 September 1960) 51. [Editorial on Behan in New York.]

Gebler, Ernest, 'At Swim-Two-Boyos', *Hibernia* (Dublin, 24 June 1977) p. 20 [Review article and Recollections of Behan.]

Gelb, Arthur, 'Brendan Behan's Sober Side', *The New York Times*, (18 September 1960) p. 3. [Interview with Behan.]

'Getting Behan Taped', *The Times Literary Supplement* (3 November

1966) p. 1000. [Review article.]

'Gift of Golden Gab', *Time* (Chicago), XCV (13 April 1970) 97. [*Borstal Boy*.]

Glanville, Brian, 'Quare Fellow Doesn't Know When to Stop', *Reynolds News* (London, 19 October 1958) p. 6. [*Borstal Boy*.]

Goldstein, Alvin H., 'An Irishman at Large', *St. Louis Post-Dispatch* (Missouri, 6 December 1964) p. 3K. [*Brendan Behan's New York*.]

Goodwin, Clive, and Tom Milne, 'Working with Joan', *Encore* (London), VII, No. 4 (July–August 1960) 9–20. [Joan Littlewood's productions of *The Quare Fellow* and *The Hostage*, passim.]

Goorney, Howard, 'Littlewood in Rehearsal', *Tulane Drama Review*, XI, No. 2 (Winter 1966) 102–103. [*The Hostage*.]

Goring, Edward, 'Ex IRA Man Returns as Poet', *Daily Mail* (London, 17 May 1956) p. 3. [Interview with Behan.]

Goulding, Cathal, 'From the Reverential to the Scurrilous', *Hibernia* (Dublin), XXXIV (7 August 1970) p. 11. [Review article.]

Gourlay, Logan, 'Show Business: The Way It Goes', *Sunday Express* (London, 24 June 1956) p. 11. [Behan's drunken appearance on BBC TV, interviewed by Malcolm Muggeridge.]

'Grab Bag of Bravado in Glimpse of Behan', *Sunday Herald Leader* (Kentucky, 30 December 1962) p. 25. [*Brendan Behan's Island*.]

Granger, Derek, 'Themes for New Voices', *The London Magazine*, III, No. 12 (December 1956) 41–47. [Evaluation of Behan and others.]

Gray, Frank, 'Back to Brendan Behan', *Sunday Tab* (Calgary, Alberta, 13 May 1979) p. T02. [Interview with Beatrice Behan.]

Gray, Tom, 'Behan Gives Readers New View of "Gotham"', *Columbus Enquirer* (Ohio, 28 December 1964) p. 8. [*Brendan Behan's New York*.]

Greacen, Robert, 'Out West', *The Listener* (London), LXVIII (4 October 1962) 527–529. [*Brendan Behan's Island*.]

——, '*Hold Your Hour and Have Another*', *The Listener* (London), LXIX (3 October 1963) 516.

Greene, Sheila, 'Dublin's Own Brendan Behan', *The Irish Digest* (Dublin), LXII, No. 4 (June 1958) 20–22. [Recollections of Behan.]

Gregor, Gordan, and Malcolm Keogh, 'Brendan Behan – He Was the Magnificent Misfit', *Daily Mirror* (London, 21 March 1964) p. 3. [Obituary.]

Grennan, Eamon, 'Brendan Behan', *The Dublin Magazine*, VI (Spring 1967) 97–98. [Review article.]

Gritten, John, 'Brutal Breeding Ground', *Daily Worker* (London, 23 October 1958) p. 2. [*Borstal Boy*.]

H., R. F., 'Behan's New York Appears', *Register-Mail* (Galesbury, Illinois, 19 November 1964). [*Brendan Behan's New York.*]

H., T., '*Hold Your Hour and Have Another*', *The Kilkenny Magazine*, No. 10 (Autumn–Winter, 1963) 121–122.

——, 'Scarperer', *Providence Sunday Journal* (Rhode Island, 12 July 1964) p. U-18. [*The Scarperer.*]

Haase, John, 'A Toast to Brendan Behan', *Los Angeles Times*, (12 July 1964) p. 15 [*The Scarperer.*]

Hackett, Walter, 'The Behan; Irish Author Knew the Strength and Failing of Art and Appetite', *The Washington. Post* (22 March 1964) Show Supplement, p. G-1. [Recollections of Behan.]

'Had a Load On', *Daily Mirror* (London, 20 June 1956) p. 5. [Behan's drunken appearance on BBC TV, interviewed by Malcolm Muggeridge.]

Haddican, James, 'Irish Stew with Behan in Kitchen', *The Times-Picayune* (New Orleans, 25 November 1962) Section 4, p. 14 [*Brendan Behan's Island.*]

——, 'Irishman Looks at Gotham', *The Times-Picayune* (New Orleans, 20 December 1964) p. 19. [*Brendan Behan's New York.*]

Hamilton, Iain, 'Among the Irish', *Encounter*, XXIII (October 1964) 36–37. [Recollections of Behan.]

Hand, Michael, 'My Life Without Brendan', *The Sunday Press* (Dublin, 20 December 1964) p. 9. [Interview with Beatrice Behan.]

Hardie, Margaret, 'Contemporary British Dramatists', *Cizí jazyky ve škole*, X (1967) 149–150. [*The Quare Fellow* and *The Hostage.*]

'Hardy Hot and Cold', *Colby Library Quarterly*, V (December 1959) 66–69. [Behan read some Hardy when he was young.]

Harmon, Maurice, 'The Era of Inhibitions: Irish Literature 1920–60', *Emory University Quarterly*, XXII, No. 1 (Spring 1966) 18–28. [Recent writers, like Behan, have shown evidence of clearing the air of 'stodgy nationalism and stale piety'.]

Harris, John, 'The Quare Fellow Says "I Was Drunk"', *Daily Herald* (London, 20 June 1956) p. 7. [Behan's drunken appearance on BBC TV, interviewed by Malcolm Muggeridge.]

Harvey, Francis, 'Brendan Behan: A Literary Re-Assessment', *Hibernia* (Dublin), XXXIII (31 January–13 February 1969) 6.

Hass, Victor Paul, 'From a Bookman's Notebook', *Omaha World-Herald*, (28 June 1964) p. 27. [*The Scarperer.*]

Hatch, Robert, 'The Roaring Presence of Brendan Behan', *Horizon* (New York), III (January 1961) 113–114. [Behan is a special type of rebel who rebels from within the world of his plays.]

Hatfield, Don, 'New York and Behan at Their Very Best', *Huntington Herald-Dispatch*, (1 November 1964) p. 35. [*Brendan Behan's New York.*]

Hawkins, Peter, 'The Genius Who Can't Stop Drinking', *Sunday Pictorial* (London, 12 July 1959) 12–13. [Behan needs proper treatment in hospital.]

Hays, H. R., 'Transcending Naturalism', *Modern Drama*, V, No. 1 (May 1962) 27–36. [Behan transcends naturalism by the use of poetic devices that reveal his attack on the Establishment.]

Hendrickx, Johan, 'The "Theatre of Fun": In Defence of Brendan Behan's *The Hostage*', *Anglo-Irish Studies*, III (1977) 85–95.

Hennigan, Aidan, 'Behan As Others Saw Him', *Evening Press* (Dublin, 21 March 1964) p. 9. [Excerpts from tributes in newspapers.]

Hewes, Henry, 'Brendan and His Double', *Saturday Review* (New York), LIII (18 April 1970) 26. [*Borstal Boy.*]

Hickey, Des, 'Ulick, You Must Be Kidding', *Sunday Independent* (Dublin, 26 July 1970) p. 21. [Review article.]

Higby, Jim, 'Late Irish Wit Wrote "Confessions of Rebel" ', *Buffalo Courier-Express*, (3 July 1966) Section D, p. 8. [*Confessions of an Irish Rebel.*]

Hogan, William, 'Brendan Behan on His Native Ireland', *San Francisco Chronicle*, (1 November 1962) p. 35. [*Brendan Behan's Island.*]

Holland, Mary, 'Brotherly Love?', *The Observer* (London, 10 October 1965) p. 27. [Review article.]

Honan, Josh, 'Brendan's Drink Problem', *The Sunday Press* (Dublin, 17 February 1974) p. 25. [Letter to the Editor.]

Honig, Nat, 'Today's Book', *Press Telegram* (Long Beach, California, 3 August 1966) p. A.33. [*Confessions of an Irish Rebel.*]

'Hostage in New York', *The Times Literary Supplement* (London, 22 October 1964) p. 955. [*Brendan Behan's New York.*]

Hughes, Marie, 'The Behan They Remember', *The Irish Press* (Dublin, 13 November 1965) p. 6. [Review article.]

Hughes, Riley, '*Borstal Boy*', *The Catholic World* (New York), CLXXXIX (May 1959) 165–166. [Review article.]

'Humanbehans', *The Times Literary Supplement*, (11 November 1965) p. 995. [*Confessions of an Irish Rebel.*] See reply by John L. Toohey, ibid, (25 November 1965) p. 1060.

Hunt, Albert, 'A Game No More', *New Society*, (8 June 1972) 524. [*The Hostage.*]

'A Hush over Dublin', *Daily Worker* (London, 23 March 1964) p. 1. [Dublin mourns Behan.]

Hutchens, John K., ' "Borstal Boy" ', *New York Herald Tribune*, (23 February 1959) p. 11. [*Borstal Boy*.]

Hynes, Sam, 'An Irish Success', *Commonweal*, LXXI, No. 23 (4 March 1960) 627–629. [Behan is preoccupied with the past but no longer believes in it.]

'I Swear I'll Beat It Yet', *The People* (London, 19 July 1959) 6. [Interview with Behan.]

Ignotus, 'Haunting Energy', *The Irish Democrat* (London, December 1963) 7. [*Hold Your Hour and Have Another*.]

' "I'm an Ass," Says Sheepish Behan', *The Toronto Daily Star* (23 March 1961) p. 35. [Behan as conferencier in the revue 'Impulse' at the O'Keefe Centre, Toronto.]

'I'm Man Who Interrupts, Cries Boisterous Behan', *The Toronto Daily Star*, (20 March 1961) p. 19. [Behan as conferencier in the revue 'Impulse' at the O'Keefe Centre, Toronto.]

'The Importance of Playwright's Vision',. *The Irish Times* (Dublin, 7 October 1967) p. 10. [Carolyn Swift on producing Behan's plays.]

'In Memory of an Immortal', *Evening Herald* (Dublin, 8 March 1974) p. 8. [A memorial plaque in memory of Behan at 14 Russell Street unveiled by Beatrice Behan.]

Inglis, Brian, 'Brendan the Gab', *The Spectator* (London, 1 November 1963) 566. [*Hold Your Hour and Have Another*.]

——, 'A Decent Man', *The Guardian* (London, 21 March 1964) p. 3. [Tribute.]

'Injured Behan's Condition Shows Slight Improvement', *The New York Times*, (31 December 1963) p. 10. [In hospital after being found unconscious on road near Dublin.]

'Invalids', *The Times* (London, 18 June 1963) p. 12. [Behan in hospital in New York.]

'Invalids', *The Times* (London, 31 December 1963) p. 10. [At Meath Hospital after being found lying in Dublin street.]

'Invalids', *The Times* (London, 1 January 1964) p. 10. [Behan in Dublin Hospital.]

'Invalids', *The Times*, (2 January 1964) p. 8.

'Invalids', *The Times* (London, 13 January 1964) p. 8.

'Invalids', *The Times* (London, 17 March 1964) p. 10.

'Invalids', *The Times* (London, 18 March 1964) p. 12.

'Invalids', *The Times* (London, 19 March 1964) p. 12.

'Invalids', *The Times* (London, 20 March 1964) p. 14.

'Irish Playwright Finds Gatskills a Haven', *Gatskill Mountain News* (Margaretville, N. Y., 4 August 1961) p. 1. [Interview with Behan.]

'Irishman on a Rampage', *Newsweek*, LIII (23 February 1959) 105–
    106. [*Borstal Boy.*]
'An Irishman on Stage', *The Economist* (London), CCLXIII (18 June
    1977) 132. [Review article.]
'It's a Sad Finale for Brendan Behan', *Catholic Standard* (Washington,
    D.C., 9 June 1966). [*Confessions of an Irish Rebel.*]
Jackman, F. P., 'A Colorful Non-Stop Talker', *Worcester Sunday
    Telegram*, (4 November 1962) p. 10E. [*Brendan Behan's Island.*]
——, 'Last from the Pen of Him', *Worcester Sunday Telegram*, (8
    November 1964) p. 10E. [*Brendan Behan's New York.*]
'Jailbreak on Old Sod Makes Amusing Story', *Sunday Call-Chronicle*
    (Allentown, Pennsylvania, 5 July 1964) p. B-9. [*The Scarperer.*]
Jeffs, Rae, 'Calamity', *The Irish Times* (Dublin, 21 March 1964) p. 9.
    [Tribute to Behan.]
Johnston, Denis, 'Behan Without the Folklore', *The Irish Times*
    (Dublin, 9 July 1977) p. 11. [Review article.]
Johnston, Jennifer, 'Courage and Loyalty', *The Sunday Times* (London,
    17 February 1974) p. 41. [Review article.]
Jones, D. A. N., 'About the Bush', *New Statesman* (London), LXVI
    (4 October 1963) 450. [*Hold Your Hour and Have Another.*]
——, 'Tamed Militant', *New Statesman* (London), LXVIII (9 October
    1964) 544. [*Brendan Behan's New York.*]
Jones, James, [Tribute], *Evening Press* (Dublin, 21 March 1964) p. 1.
Jordan, John, 'Behan', *Hibernia* (Dublin), XXVIII (April 1964) 13.
    [Tribute to and recollections of Behan.]
——, 'Lest We Forget', *Hibernia* (Dublin, 21 January 1977) p. 17.
    [Recollections of Behan.]
——, 'More About Behan', *Hibernia* (Dublin, 4 February 1977) p. 29.
    [Recollections of Behan.]
'Jottings by Man about Town', *Dublin Evening Mail*, (5 July 1956)
    p. 4. [Behan's drunken appearance on BBC TV, interviewed by
    Malcolm Muggeridge.]
'Journalism', *The Times Literary Supplement* (London, 27 September
    1963) p. 774. [*Hold Your Hour and Have Another.*]
Joyce, C. A., 'The Behan I Knew Was So Gentle', *The Sunday Press*
    (Dublin, 5 April 1964 p. 12. [Recollections of Behan by the
    former Governor of Hollesley Bay Borstal Institution.]
'Just Deserts', *Plays and Players* (London), VII, No. 4 (January 1960)
    20. [*The Hostage*, passim.]
Kavanagh, Sean, 'Brendan Behan', *The Irish Times* (Dublin, 30 July
    1970) p. 11. [Letter to the Editor defending Behan from charges

of homosexuality made by his biographer Ulick O'Connor.]

Kazin, Alfred, 'The Causes Go, the Rebels Remain', *Atlantic Monthly* (Boston), CCIII (June 1959) 65–67. Reprinted in *Contemporaries* (Boston: Little, Brown, 1962) pp. 240–246. [*Borstal Boy.*]

Keane, F. J., 'Behan's-Eye View', *Irish Independent* (Dublin, 13 October 1962) p. 10. [*Brendan Behan's Island.*]

Keane, John B., 'Behan', *The Sunday Press* (Dublin, 10 October 1965) p. 17. [Review article.]

Kearney, Colbert, '*Borstal Boy*: A Portrait of the Artist as a Young Prisoner', *Ariel: A Review of International English Literature* (Calgary, Alberta), VII, No. 2 (April 1976) 47–62.

Keelan, B. C. L., 'The Stout Fellow', *The Tablet* (London, 13 October 1962) 960. [*Brendan Behan's Island.*]

——, 'Being Behan', *The Tablet* (London, 23 November 1963) 1268. [*Hold Your Hour and Have Another.*]

Kelly, Bernard, 'New Behan Book: Intimate, Funny', *Denver Post*, (4 December 1962) p. 25 [*Brendan Behan's Island.*]

——, 'Early Behan Novel Lacks Later Touch', *The Sunday Denver Post*, (5 July 1964) p. 10. [*The Scarperer.*]

——, ' "Confessions" 100-Proof Behan', *Denver Post* (Colorado, 5 September 1966) p. 25. [*Confessions of an Irish Rebel.*]

Kelly, Henry, 'The Fat and the Lean', *Hibernia* (Dublin), XXX (October 1966) 18. [Review article.]

Kelly, J. W., 'Ulick Is Pleased by Send-Off', *Sunday Independent* (Dublin, 26 July 1970) p. 7. [London reception of the first biography of Behan by Ulick O'Connor.]

Kelly, Seamus, 'Where Motley Is Worn', *The Spectator* (London), CXCVI (20 April 1956) 538, 540. [*The Quare Fellow.*]

——, 'Behan Was Dublin's Own – the Essence of a Joycean Character', *The Irish Times* (Dublin, 21 March 1964) p. 9. [Tribute to Behan.]

Kennedy, Maurice, 'Budding Genius', *The Irish Times* (Dublin, 14 September 1963) p. 8. [*Hold Your Hour and Have Another.*]

Kennedy, William, 'The Masked Ball: Mr. Behan', *Look*, XXXV (4 May 1971) 76. [Review article.]

Kennelly, Brendan, 'Behan – Wonder and Waste', *Sunday Independent* (Dublin, 26 July 1970) p. 21. [Review article.]

——, 'Comic, Compassionate, Unique', *The Times Higher Education Supplement* (London, 21 October 1977) p. 12. [Review article.]

Kenny, Sean, 'Great Man., *Evening Press* (Dublin, 21 March 1964) p. 9. [Recollections of Behan.]

Keown, Don, 'Irish Rebel Pays Tribute to a City', *Independent Journal*
(San Rafael, California, 31 October 1964) p. M14. [*Brendan
Behan's New York.*]
——, 'Brendan Behan! Last Defiance of the Conventions of Society',
Independent Journal (San Rafael, California, 28 May 1966).
[*Confessions of an Irish Rebel.*]
Kiely, Benedict, 'Rich in Talent and a Great Personality; Brendan
Behan Gave Us Many Happy Hours', *Sunday Press* (Dublin, 22
March 1964) p. 6. [Recollections of Behan.]
——, 'That Old Triangle: A Memory of Brendan Behan', *The Hollins
Critic* (Hollins College, Virginia), II, No. 1 (February 1965) 1–12.
Reprinted in *The Sounder Few: Essays From the 'Hollins Critic'*, ed.
R. H. W. Dillard, George Garrett, and John R. Moore (Athens,
Georgia: University of Georgia Press, 1971) pp. 85–99. [Behan as
a gregarious man, a garrulous man, a kindly man, and a true
comic.]
——, 'The Great Gazebo', *Eire-Ireland* (St. Paul, Minnesota), II, No.
4 (Winter 1967) 85–86. [Behan and the theme in Irish literature
of the great houses of the landed classes.]
Kilroy, Thomas, '*The Hostage*', *Studies; An Irish Quarterly Review*
(Dublin), XLVIII, No. 189 (Spring 1959) 111–112.
——, 'Groundwork for an Irish Theatre', *Studies; An Irish Quarterly
Review* (Dublin), XLVIII, 190 (Summer 1959), 192–198.
['Brendan Behan could not . . . be considered representative of a
whole new movement in Irish writing.']
King, Jim, 'Brendan Behan Goes on the Wagon', *Today* (London), I,
No. 24 (6 August 1960) 25–26. [Interview with Behan.]
——, 'It's Not For the Booze', *The Irish Digest* (Dublin), LXIX, No. 4
(October 1960) 15. [The changes which sobriety has wrought in
Behan.]
King, Louise W., 'Talking Around New York', *The Sunday Times*
(London, 27 September 1964) p. 48. [*Brendan Behan's New York.*]
Kinross, Lord, 'One or Two Jars in New York', *The Sunday
Telegraph* (London, 27 September 1964) p. 22. [*Brendan Behan's
New York.*]
Kitching, Jessie, 'Capsules', *New York Post* (8 November 1964) p. 47.
[*Brendan Behan's New York.*]
Klarfeld, Jonathan M., 'An Irish Pub Crawl In New York', *Holyoke
Transcript-Telegram* (Massachusetts, 14 November 1964) p. 12.
[*Brendan Behan's New York.*]
Kleinstück, Johannes, 'Brendan Behan's "The Hostage" ', *Essays and*

Studies by Members of the English Association (London), XXIV
(1971) 69–82.
Knight, G. Wilson, 'The Kitchen Sink; On Recent Developments in
Drama', *Encounter*, XXI, No. 6 (December 1963) 48–54. [Modern
dramatists are breaking new ground, with reference to *The Quare
Fellow*.]
Kohler, Peter, 'New York As Behan Lived It', *Charlotte Observer* (North
Carolina, 22 November 1964) Section C, p. 2. [*Brendan Behan's
New York*.]
Koziol, Herbert, 'Zur Literarischen Verwendung des Rhyming Slang',
Archiv für Das Studium Die Neveren Sprachen und Literatur, CXVII
(August 1965) 105–108. [Rhyming slang in *Borstal Boy*.]
Krause, David, 'The Barbarous Sympathies of Antic Irish Comedy',
The Malahat Review, XXII (April 1972) 99–117 passim.
Lagerlöf, Olof, 'Dikt och förbannad lögn [A pack of lies]', Vecko-
Journalen (Stockholm, 16 October 1959) 26, 63–65.
[Recollections of Behan.]
Lambert, J. W., 'The London Theatre', *International Theatre Annual*, II
(1956–7) 11–38. [*The Quare Fellow*.]
——, 'The Season's Work: London', *International Theatre Annual*, IV
(1958–9) 14–51. [*The Hostage*.]
Landstone, Charles, 'From John Osborne to Shelagh Delaney', *World
Theatre*, VIII, No. 3 (Autumn 1959) 203–216 passim.
'Large, Rumpled and Belligerent', *TV Guide* (Philadelphia, 28 January
1961) 22–23. [Interview with Behan.]
Larsen, Richard B., 'Behan Adds a Poet's Touch to Spectacle of New
York', *The Atlanta Journal*, (8 November 1964) p. 12-D. [*Brendan
Behan's New York*.]
'The Last Years of Brendan', *The Sunday Express* (London, 30 October
1966) p. 6. [Review article.]
'Latest Wills', *The Times* (London, 23 April 1966) p. 12. [Behan left
only £2,136.]
'Laughter Left to Us in Book and Plays', *The Irish Times* (Dublin, 21
March 1964) p. 9. [Obituary.]
Leonard, Hugh, 'Greatest Dublin Jackeen', *Plays and Players* (London),
XI, No. 8 (May 1964) 43. [Recollections and evaluation of
Behan.]
——, 'Behan's Talent was Inhibited by Law!', *Sunday Independent*
(Dublin, 19 June 1977) p. 25. [Review article.]
L[eventhal], A. J., '*The Quare Fellow* by Brendan Behan', *The Dublin
Magazine*, XXXII, No. 1 (January–March 1957) 52–53.

Levidova, I., 'A New Hero Appears in the Theatre (Notes on Young Dramatists in England)', *Inostrannaya Literatura* [Foreign Literature], VIII, No. 1 (January 1962) 201–208. [The 'plebeian' hero in Behan and others. In Russian.]

Levin, Milton, 'The Major Works of Brendan Behan', *Eire-Ireland* (St. Paul, Minnesota), X, No. 2 (Summer 1975) 143–144. [Review article.]

Levine, Paul, 'Individualism and the Traditional Talent', *Hudson Review*, XVII (Autumn 1964) 470–477. [*The Scarperer*.]

Levitt, Paul M., 'Hostages to History: Title as Dramatic Metaphor in *The Hostage*', *Die Neueren Sprachen* (Frankfurt), XXIV (October 1975) 401–406. ['The title of the play has several meanings and provides a key to understanding Behan's attitude toward tradition and, in particular, the relation of past to present.'.]

Liddy, James, 'Te Deum for Joyce; Imitated from the Irish of Brendan Behan', *The Holy Door* (Dublin), No. 3 (Spring 1966) 16. [A poem.]

'Like Sitting on a Tornado', *RTE Guide* (Dublin, 8 February 1974) 7. [Recollections of Behan.]

Linehan, Fergus, 'Four Irish Playwrights', *The Irish Digest* (Dublin), LXXIV, No. 2 (April 1962) 84–87. [Abroad, Behan is Ireland's most popular playwright; but at home, that distinction goes to John B. Keane.]

——, 'Brendan in the New World', *The Irish Times* (Dublin, 24 October 1964) p. 8. [*Brendan Behan's New York*.]

Littlewood, Joan, 'It Is the End of an Epoch', *Sunday Independent* (Dublin, 22 March 1964) p. 7. Also in *The Observer* (London, 22 March 1964) p. 3. [Tribute to Behan.]

——, 'Behan's Unbodied Soul', *The Irish Press* (Dublin, 14 July 1977) p. 6. [Review article and recollections of Behan.]

Logue, Christopher, 'What Happened to Ginger?', *New Statesman* (London), LVI (25 October 1958) 566–567. [*Borstal Boy*.]

'London Diary: The Quare Fellow', *The Northern Whig* (Belfast, 20 June 1956) p. 2. [Behan's drunken appearance on BBC TV, interviewed by Malcolm Muggeridge.]

London Pressmen "Kidnapped" Playwright Behan!', *Evening Press* (Dublin, 20 June 1956) p. 1. [Before leaving London for Dublin after success of *The Quare Fellow*.]

Lord, Graham, 'Outrageous, but So Warm-Hearted', *The Sunday Express* (London, 10 October 1965) p. 6. [Review article.]

'The Lord High Executioner', *Atlantic Monthly* (Boston), CC (October

1957) 180–181. [*The Quare Fellow.*]

Lucas, Brock, 'Early Borstal Boy', *St. Petersburg Times* (Florida, 28 June 1964) p. 5. [*The Scarperer.*]

Lusty, Robert, '*Borstal Boy*', *The Spectator* (London, 21 November 1958) p. 703. [Letter to the Editor.]

Lynch, Brendan, 'The Other Side of Brendan Behan', *Irish Socialist* (Dublin), No. 36 (May 1964) 2, 4. [Obituary and recollections.]

Lyons, Leonard, 'The Lyons Den', *New York Post Magazine*, (11 December 1960) 7. [Recollections of Behan.]

M., M., 'An Echo of Brendan Behan', *People's World* (San Francisco), (27 August 1966). [*Confessions of an Irish Rebel.*]

M., T., 'An Exasperating Irish Puck', *The Houston Chronicle*, (21 October 1962) p. 15 [*Brendan Behan's Island.*]

MacAlernon, Don, '*Brendan Behan's Island: An Irish Sketchbook*', *Focus; A Monthly Review* (Belfast), V (December 1962) 283.

——, 'Beckett and Behan', *Focus; A Monthly Review* (Belfast), VI (February 1963) 45–46. [Review article.]

——, '*Hold Your Hour and Have Another*', *Focus; A Monthly Review* (Belfast), VI (November 1963) 262.

MacAnna, Tomás, 'The Villon of Dublin', *The Times Literary Supplement*, (15 July 1977) p. 850. [Review article.]

MacAonghusa, Proinsias, 'Was Poet, Comedian, Rebel and Lover of People', *Sunday Independent* (Dublin, 22 March 1964) p. 7. [Recollections of Behan.]

——, 'Passing of Stephen B.', *New Statesman* (London), LXXIV (21 July 1967) 82–83. [An account of the wake for Brendan's father.]

McCartin, James T., 'Irish Without Tears', *The Reporter*, (New York), XXVIII (31 January 1963) 56. [*Brendan Behan's Island.*]

MacColl, René, 'A Brain Hit by a Bottle', *Daily Express* (London, 21 March 1964) p. 5. [Tribute to and recollections of Behan.]

MacCormack, Joseph, 'When Behan, of Emerald Isle, Visited Staten', *Staten Island Sunday Advance*, (7 March 1965) p. 9. [Recollections of Behan.]

McCoy, Martha B., 'Mixture of Things Gaelic', *Chattanooga Times* (Tennessee, 2 December 1962). [*Brendan Behan's Island.*]

McCreesh, Gerard, 'Behan Eludes Documentary', *Irish Independent* (Dublin, 8 April 1971) p. 8. [Film on Behan on BBC TV programme 'Omnibus'.]

McCullough, David, '*Confessions of an Irish Rebel*', *Book-of-the-Month Club News*, (May 1966) 10.

MacDonagh, Donagh, 'Behans Abroad', *The Kilkenny Magazine*, Nos.

12–13 (Spring 1965) 55–60. [*Brendan Behan's New York*.]

McE, F., '*Brendan Behan's Island – An Irish Sketch Book*', *The Kilkenny Magazine*, No. 9 (Spring 1963) 85–87.

MacInnes, Colin, 'The Writings of Brendan Behan', *The London Magazine*, II, No. 5 (August 1962) 53–61. [Reassessment.]

——, 'More about Brendan', *The Observer* (London, 13 November 1966) p. 26. [*The Scarperer*.]

MacIntyre, Tom, 'This Dying Lark', *Kenyon Review*, XXVII (Winter 1965) 152–155. [Evaluation of Behan's work.]

——, 'Brendan', *Saturday Review* (New York), LIV (1 May 1971) 37. [Review article.]

McKee, John DeWitt, '*Brendan Behan's Island*', *Sun Dial* (El Paso, Texas, 28 October 1962).

McKeever, Thomas, 'A Touch of the Drama – Irish Style', *The Sunday Press* (Dublin, 30 August 1970) p. 16. [Attack on Behan for helping 'to perpetuate the stage Irishman image'.] See reply by Harry J. MacMurrough-Kavanagh, ibid., (6 September 1970) p. 16.

McKenna, Siobhán, 'One Day I Met Brendan Behan', *The Irish Times* (Dublin, 21 March 1964) p. 9. [Tribute to Behan.]

McKenzie, Alice, '*Confessions of an Irish Rebel*', *Clearwater Sun* (Florida, 29 May 1966) p. 7-D.

McKiernan, Eóin, 'The World of Brendan Behan', *Eire-Ireland* (St. Paul, Minnesota), I, No. 4 (Winter 1966) 98. [Review article.]

McKnight, Gerald, 'How I Stay Married to Mr. Mitchum', *Sunday Mirror* (London, 26 January 1964) pp. 22–23. [Interview with Beatrice Behan.]

MacLochlainn, Alf, 'Behan's Life Told with Compassion', *Irish Independent* (Dublin, 23 July 1970) p. 10. [Review article.] See reply by 'Dands', ibid., (29 July 1970) p. 8.

MacMahon, Bryan, 'Brendan Behan: Vital Human Being; A Memoir', *The North American Review*, I, No. 2 (Summer 1964) 60–64.

McMahon, Seán, 'Brendan Behan', *Eire-Ireland* (St. Paul, Minnesota), I, No. 4 (Winter 1966) 97–98. [*The Scarperer*.]

——, 'The Quare Fellow', *Eire-Ireland* (St. Paul, Minnesota), IV, No. 4 (Winter 1969) 143–157. [Evaluation of Behan as a writer.]

——, 'Brendan Behan', *Eire-Ireland* (St. Paul, Minnesota), VI, No. 2 (Summer 1971) 180–182. [Review article.]

MacManus, Francis, 'Brendan Behan', *The Irish Press* (Dublin, 4 April 1964) p. 6. [Recollections of Behan.]

MacManus, Patricia, 'A Wild Boyo Exuberantly Sweeps Through

Eire', *New York Herald Tribune Books*, (7 July 1963) p. 6. [*Brendan Behan's Island.*]

MacNamara, Desmond, 'Saints and Ladders', *New Statesman* (London), LXX (5 November 1965) 705. [*Confessions of an Irish Rebel.*]

———, 'Early and Late', *New Statesman* (London), LXXII (18 November 1966) 750. [*The Scarperer.*]

———, 'The Biggest Heart in Ireland', *The Tablet* (London, 17 December 1977) pp. 1201–1202. [Review article.]

MacNamara, Helen, ' "I'm the Fella Who Interrupts" ', *The Telegram* (Toronto, 20 March 1961) p. 32. [Behan as conferencier at 'Impulse!' at the O'Keefe Centre, Toronto.]

McNeela, Paddy, and Sean O'Briain, 'Brendan Behan', *The Irish Times* (Dublin, 27 July 1970) p. 11. [Letter to the editor defending Behan from charges of homosexuality made by his biographer Ulick O'Connor.]

MacNeice, Louis, 'The Two Faces of Ireland', *The Observer* (London, 30 September 1962) p. 29. [*Brendan Behan's Island.*]

Maher, Mary, 'Leaf Out of Behan's Book to Promote Hall for Crumlin Community', *The Irish Times* (Dublin, 9 June 1975) p. 13. [A bronze plaque head of Behan unveiled at 70 Kildare Road, Crumlin, Dublin.]

Mahon, Derek, 'The Gaelic Behan', *The Times* (London, 25 July 1970) p. 8. [Review article.]

Malcolm, Donald, 'The Ballad of Borstal Gaol', *New Yorker*, XXXV, No. 20 (4 July 1959) 69–72. [*Borstal Boy.*]

Malin, Brendan, 'Playwright Backs Jack; Slim, Boozeless Behan Drinks in Hub Skyline', *Boston Evening Globe*, (2 September 1960) p. [Interview with Behan.]

———, 'Behan Unpolished', *Boston Globe*, (26 June 1966) p. A24. [*Confessions of an Irish Rebel.*]

Mando, 'Irischer Querkopf und Dichter Brendan Behan: "Ich Mache, was ich will!" ', *B. Z.* (Berlin, 14 March 1959) p. 8. [Behan as a 'contrary' poet.]

Manning, Mary, 'The Behan Legend', *The Irish Times* (Dublin, 9 February 1974) p. 10. [Review article.] See correspondence by Leslie Gillespie and Robert Greacen, ibid, (14 February 1974) p. 11; by Mary Manning, ibid, (19 February 1974) p. 11; and by Leslie Curtis, ibid, (23 February 1974) p. 13.

'Marcel on Behan', *Hibernia* (Dublin), XXIII (June 1959) 7. [Gabriel Marcel on *The Quare Fellow* and *The Hostage.*]

Marcus, Steven, 'Tom Brown in Quod', *Partisan Review*, XXVI, No. 2
    (Spring 1959) 335–344. [*Borstal Boy.*]
Marowitz, Charles, 'New Wave in a Dead Sea', *X: A Quarterly Review*,
    I (1960) 270–277. [The Theatre of Social Realism in London:
    Behan and others.]
Marriott, R. B., 'Brendan Behan – Brace, Honest and True', *The Stage
    and Television Today* (London, 26 March 1964) p. 6. [Tribute.]
Marron, Kevin, ' "I Was So Wrong about Him" ', *The Sunday Press*
    (Dublin, 19 July 1970) p. 17. [Interview with Ulick O'Connor,
    Behan's biographer.]
Martin, Augustine, 'Brendan Behan', *Threshold* (Belfast), No. 18 (1943)
    22–28. [*The Quare Fellow* and *The Hostage.*]
——, 'At the Shaky Man's ', *The Irish Press* (Dublin, 12 November
    1966) p. 6. [*The Scarperer.*]
Martin, Eamonn, 'Brendan Behan's Quare World', *The Globe Magazine*
    (Toronto, 15 September 1962) 4–6. [Interview with Behan.]
Mathieson, Andrew, 'The Dark East', *Drama* (London), No. 93
    (Summer 1969) 45–49. [Behan and Stratford East productions of
    The Hostage and *The Quare Fellow.*]
Mauel, Ed., 'Looking at Behan Two Ways', *Sunday Press-Enterprise*
    (Riverside, California, 4 September 1966) p. C-10. [*Confessions of
    an Irish Rebel.*]
Maulnier, Thierry, 'Un otage', *Revue de Paris*, XILX (March 1962)
    152–155. [*The Hostage.*]
Melville, Frank, 'Talk with the Author', *Newsweek*, LIII (23 February
    1959) 106. [Interview with Behan.]
Merwin, W. S., 'Laughter and the Cage', *The Nation* (New York),
    CLXXXI (28 February 1959) 190–191. [*Borstal Boy.*]
Mhaol, An Fhirinne, 'The Borstal Boy', *The United Irishman* (Dublin),
    XVI (May 1964) 11. [Tribute to Behan.]
Miller, Liam, '*The Quare Fellow*', *Irish Writing* (Dublin), No. 36
    (Autumn–Winter 1956) 189–190.
Millf, Phil, 'Behan Rates Above College Scholars', *Pensacola Journal*,
    (22 May 1966). [*Confessions of an Irish Rebel.*]
Mercier, Vivian, 'The Dublin Tradition', *New Republic* (New York),
    CXXXV (6 August 1956), 21–22. [*The Quare Fellow* is a play
    'which some regard as the most original Irish play for years'.]
Mills, John A., 'Beckett and Behan', *The Quarterly Journal of Speech*,
    LII (1966) 404–405. [Review article.]
Miner, Virginia Scott, 'And All Those Behans, Too', *Kansas City Star*,
    (8 May 1966) p. 6F. [Review article.]

Mitchell, Adrian, '*The Quare Fellow*', *The London Magazine*, IV, No. 8 (August 1957) 77–79.

Mitchell, Harry, 'Television: BBC Last Night', *Evening Chronicle* (Manchester, 19 June 1956) p. 5. [Behan's drunken appearance on BBC TV, interviewed by Malcolm Muggeridge.]

Mitchell, Louis D., 'Beatrice Behan: *My Life with Brendan*', *Best Sellers* (Scranton, Pennsylvania), XXXIV (1 December 1974) 386–387. [Review article.]

Moore, Brian, 'The Quare Fellow Scapa-Flowed', *Book Week* (*New York Herald Tribune*, 21 June 1964) pp. 3, 14. [*The Scarperer*.]

——, 'A Stage Irish Drunk Who Died of Drink', *New York Times Book Review*, (25 April 1971) p. 35. [Review article.]

Moseley, Virginia, 'A Week in Dublin', *Modern Drama*, IV No. 2 (September 1961) 164–171. [Behan participating in a panel discussion on Irish Drama.]

'Mother and Baby Are Very Comfortable', *Evening Herald* (Dublin, 26 November 1963) p. 7. [Blanaid Behan born for Brendan and Beatrice Behan.]

Moynihan, John, 'Manhattan Manners', *The Sunday Telegraph* (London, 13 November 1966) p. 15. [*The Scarperer*.]

'Mr. Behan Feels Fine', *Evening Standard* (London, 19 June 1956) p. 4 [Behan's drunken appearance on BBC TV, interviewed by Malcolm Muggeridge.]

'Mr. Behan in a Coma', *The Irish Press* (Dublin, 16 March 1964) p. 1. [In Dublin hospital.]

'Mr. Behan Takes the Stage', *The Manchester Guardian*, (13 July 1959) p. 12. [Behan entertains travellers to an hour's recital of ballads at London Airport when his plane to Dublin is delayed.]

'Mr. Brendan Behan', *The Times* (London, 1 April 1960) p. 6. [At Middlesex Hospital, London.]

'Mr. Brendan Behan in Hospital', *The Times* (London, 31 March 1960) p. 12. [At Middlesex Hospital, London.]

'Mr. Brendan Behan Seriously Ill', *The Times* (London, 16 March 1964) p. 10. [At Meath Hospital, Dublin.]

'Mr. Brendan Behan: The Quare Fellow', *The Times* (London, 21 March 1964) p. 12. [Obituary.]

'Mr. Stephen Behan; A Dublin Character', *The Times* (London, 15 July 1967) p. 12. [Obituary of Behan's father.]

'Mrs. Beatrice Behan', *The Irish Times* (Dublin, 26 November 1963) p. 8. [Gives birth to Blanaid Behan.]

'Mrs. Behan's Own Story', *The State and Television Today* (London, 21

September 1972) p. 23. [Leslie Frewin to publish Beatrice Behan's life with Brendan.]

Muggeridge, Malcolm, 'Brendan Behan at Lime Grove', *New Statesman* (London), LXVII (27 March 1964) 488. [Recollections of interview with Behan in 'Panorama' series on BBC TV on 18 June 1956.]

Mulchrone, Vincent, 'Drunk? Sure, I'd Had a Bottle, Says the Quare TV Man', *Daily Mail* (London, 20 June 1956) p. 1. [Interview with Behan.]

Mullane, Dermot, 'The Famous and the Unknown at Brendan Behan's Funeral', *The Irish Times* (Dublin, 24 March 1964) p. 4.

Murdoch, John, 'The Behan I Knew Was So Gentle, Says the Man Who Was His Borstal Boss', *The Sunday Press*, (Dublin, 5 April 1964) p. 12. [Interview with C. A. Joyce, the former Governor of Hollesley Bay Borstal Institution.]

Murphy, Brian, 'Brendan Behan at Theatre Workshop: Story-Teller into Playwright', *Prompt* (London), V (1964) 4–8. The author, who appeared in Theatre Workshop's productions of both *The Quare Fellow* and *The Hostage*, discusses the extent of the contributions of Joan Littlewood and of the cast.]

'*My Brother Brendan*', *New York Times Book Review*, (10 April 1966) p. 22. [Review article.]

'*My Life with Brendan*', *The Times* (London, 28 February 1974) p. 15. [Brief review article.]

'The Mystery of Behan: Was Lying in Pool of Blood', *Evening Press* (Dublin, 30 December 1963) p. 1. [Behan found unconscious on roadway.]

Nadeau, Maurice, 'Souvenirs', *L'Express* (Paris, 22 December 1960) pp. 29–30. [*Borstal Boy*.]

Na Gopaleen, Myles, See O'Nolan, Brian.

Nathan, David, 'This Man Behan', *Daily Herald* (London, 21 March 1964) p. 3. [Recollections of Behan.]

Near, George, '*Brendan Behan's New York*', *Herald Banner* (Greenville, Texas, 22 November 1964) p. B2.

'New Behan Book Proves Interesting Surprise', *The Sunday Star* (Washington, D.C., 11 November 1962) p. B5. [*Brendan Behan's Island*.]

'New Book on Brendan Behan by Ulick', *Sunday Independent* (Dublin, 12 July 1970) p. 11. [Ulick O'Connor on how he researched for his biography on Behan.]

'New Fiction', *The Times* (London, 1 December 1966) p. 16. [*The Scarperer.*]

Newquist, Roy, '*Confessions of an Irish Rebel*', *Chicago's American*, (29 May 1966).

'News in Brief: Eire Book Ban', *The Times* (London, 12 November 1958) p. 6. [*Borstal Boy* banned by the Censorship and Publications Board of the Republic of Ireland.]

Nichols, Lewis, 'A Behan Wake', *New York Times Book Review*, (22 May 1966) p. 8. [*Confessions of an Irish Rebel.*]

'The Night Behan Was Not Himself', *Daily Herald* (London, 15 October 1958) p. 2. [Recollections of Behan.]

'No Clues to Behan Wound Mystery', *The Irish Press* (Dublin, 31 December 1963) p. 1. [Behan found unconscious on roadway.]

Noble, Arthur, Howard Wantuch, and Sidney Kline, 'Behan Back on Booze Binge; Goes Into Orbit in Theatre', *Daily News* (New York, 27 October 1960) pp. 3, 80. [Interview with Behan.]

'Noisy Binge Jails Behan', *Toronto Daily Star*, (22 March 1961) p. 1. [Behan charged with assault and causing a disturbance.]

Nolan, James, 'Written for Export', *Newark News*, (18 November 1962) Section 4, p. 14. [*Brendan Behan's Island.*]

Nores, Dominique, 'Reconnaissance de Brendan Behan', *Les Lettres Nouvelles* (Paris, October 1962) 132–137. [An attempt to understand Behan the man.]

'Notes by Sage of Nonsense', *The Globe and Mail* (Toronto, 18 March 1961) p. 13. [Interview with Behan.]

'Now Life Comes Into Focus for the Quare Fellow; Behan Avoids the Ould Stuff', *Daily Mail* (London, 28 August 1956) p. 3. [Interview with Behan.]

Nye, Robert, 'The Shadow of a Brother', *Tribune* (London, 3 December 1965) p. 13. [Review article.]

Oberbeck, S. K., 'From Dublin to Derry', *St. Louis Post Dispatch* (Missouri, 14 October 1962) p. 4B [*Brendan Behan's Island.*]

——, 'Saint Brendan of the Prodigal', *Book World* (*Chicago Tribune*, 17 March 1968) pp. 4–5. [Review article.]

O'Briain, Sean, 'In Jail with Brendan Behan', *The Irish Press* (Dublin, 21 May 1964) p. 8. [Recollections of Behan.]

——, 'I Knew Brendan Behan', *The Kerryman* (Tralee, 23 May 1964) pp. 6–7. [Recollections of Behan.]

O'Brien, Conor, 'Death or Transfiguration?', *The Tablet* (London, 7 February 1959) 133–134. [*The Hostage.*]

O'Brien, Frank, 'Another Revolution: Modern Poetry in Irish', *Eire-*

Ireland, I (Winter 1966) 13–22 [On the basis of Behan's few
Gaelic poems, he is considered one of the major poets of his gene-
ration writing in Irish.]

O'Brien, John H., 'Behan Weaves Way Through His Ireland', *Detroit
News* (Michigan, 18 November 1962) p. 3G. [*Brendan Behan's
Island.*]

———, 'And a Behan Potboiler', *The Detroit News*, (7 June 1964)
p. 3G. [*The Scarperer.*]

O'Brien, Kate, 'Irish Genius', *New Statesman* (London), LXVII (27
March 1964) 488. [Tribute to and evaluation of Behan.]

O'Casey, Sean, 'He Had So Much to Offer', *Irish Independent* (Dublin,
21 March 1964) p. 14. [Tribute to Behan.]

———, 'He Ran Too Quickly', *Evening Press* (Dublin, 21 March 1964)
p. 1. [Tribute to Behan.]

O Conghaola, Le Sean, 'Breandon O Beachain sa Chaeltacht', *Inniu*
(Dublin, 20 January 1967) p. 2. [Behan in Gaelic-speaking
districts.]

O'Connell, Jerry, 'Drunken Genius', *The Catholic World*, CCXIII
(September 1971) 296–297. [Review article.]

O'Connor, Frank, ' "To Show That Still She Lives" ', *Chicago Sunday
Tribune*, (1 March 1959) p. 3. [*Borstal Boy.*]

———, 'He Was So Much Larger Than Life', *Sunday Independent*
(Dublin, 22 March 1964) p. 7. [Recollections of Behan.]

O'Connor, Philip, 'Writing in Class', *Antioch Review*, XIX, No. 2
(Summer 1959) 271–276. [Fusion of 'mass entertainment' and
'traditional culture' in Behan and others.]

O'Donnell, Donat, 'Queer World', *The Spectator* (London, 7 November
1958) 620. [*Borstal Boy.*]

O'Dowling, Elsie, 'The Last of Brendan Behan', *The Irish Democrat*
(London, December 1965) 7. [*Confessions of an Irish Rebel.*]

O Duhb, Cathal, '*Borstal Boy*', *The Irish Democrat* (London, October
1958) 7.

O'Faolain, Sean, 'Love of Life Was the Kiss of Death', *New York
Times Book Review*, (26 June 1966) p. 7. [*Confessions of an Irish
Rebel.*]

O'Farrell, Mairin, 'A Dublin Literary Pub', *Hibernia* (Dublin),
XXVIII (July–August 1964) 12–13. [Recollections of Behan and
other writers by Paddy O'Brien, head barman of McDaid's.]

O'Flynn, Criostoir, 'Play-Doctors', *The Irish Times* (Dublin, 10
October 1967) p. 9. [Letter to the Editor on Carolyn Swift and
The Quare Fellow.]

O Glaisne, Risteárd, '*The Hostage*', *Focus; A monthly Review* (Belfast), II (February 1959) 28–29.
——, 'Breandán dar le Ulick', *Comhar* (Dublin), XXIX, No. 12 (December 1970) 23–24. [Review article.]
O hAilpín, Pádraic, 'Dé Bheatha', *The Irish Press* (Dublin, 4 April 1964) p. 6. [Tribute to Behan in verse.]
Ó hAodha, Micheál, 'Theatre in Dublin', *The Irish Press* (Dublin, 24 November 1962) p. 4. [Review article.]
——, 'Delighted', *The Irish Times* (Dublin, 21 March 1964) pp. 1, 9. [Tribute to Behan.]
——, 'A Tribute to Brendan Behan', *RTV Guide* (Dublin), II (1 May 1964) 7.
——, 'Behan the Ballader', *The Irish Times* (Dublin, 22 March 1974) p. 10. [Recollections of Behan.]
O'Hara, Mary, 'Gael Warnings Flutter', *Pittsburgh Press* (21 October 1962) Section 5, p. 10 [*Brendan Behan's Island*.]
O'Keefe, Timothy, 'Borstal Boy', *The Times Educational Supplement* (London, 5 August 1977) p. 13. [Review article.]
O'Kelly, Seamus G., 'The Brendan Behan I Knew', *Evening Herald* (Dublin, 31 March 1964) p. 9. [Recollections of Behan.]
——, 'Brendan as I Knew Him', *Evening Herald* (Dublin, 1 April 1964) p. 4. [Recollections of Behan.]
——, 'Brendan', *Evening Herald* (Dublin, 2 April 1964) p. 6. [Recollections of Behan.]
——, 'I Knew the Real Brendan Behan', *The Irish Digest* (Dublin), LXXVIII, No. 12 (June 1964) 67–70. [Recollections of Behan.]
——, 'Brendan Behan the Rebel', *Evening Herald* (Dublin, 2 December 1965) p. 10. [Letter to the Editor on Behan and the Irish Republican Movement.]
'Old School Noose', *Time*, LXXIII (9 March 1959) 86–87. [Review article.]
'Old-Fashioned Adventure', *The Sioux City Sunday Journal* (12 July 1964) p. C4. [*The Scarperer*.]
O Luanaigh, Liam, 'O Beachain: Dha Leabhar Eile', *Inniu* (Dublin, 14 April 1967) p. 2. [Review article.]
O'Neill, John Drew, 'Brendan Go Bragh!', *Michigan Quarterly Review*, IV, No. 1 (Winter 1965) 19–22. [Recollections of Behan.]
O'Neill-Barna, Anne, 'Unreconstructed Rebel', *New York Times Book Review*, (4 November 1962) p. 5. [*Brendan Behan's Island*.]
——, 'In the Snug of a Pub', *New York Times Book Review*, (2 February 1964) p. 7. [*Hold Your Hour and Have Another*.]

66   BRENDAN BEHAN: ANNOTATED BIBLIOGRAPHY OF CRITICISM

O'Neill-Barna, Anne, 'Himself at All Times', *New York Times Book
Review*, (21 June 1964) p. 5. [*The Scarperer.*]
——, 'A Sort of One-Man Melting Pot', *New York Times Book Review*,
(15 November 1964) p. 6. [*Brendan Behan's New York.*]
O'Nolan, Brian [Myles Na Gopaleen], 'Behanism', *The Irish Times*
(Dublin, 23 July 1956) p. 6. [Recollections of Behan.]
'Order Behan Arrest', *The Toronto Daily Star*, (27 March 1961) Section
IV, p. 1. [Behan arrested in Toronto after failure to appear in
court on charges of assault.]
O'Reilly, Michael, 'Brendan – the Human Behan', *The Irish Digest*
(Dublin), LXXVII, No. 3 (May 1963) 15–18. [Interview with
Behan.]
O'Riordan, John, 'A Quare and a Rare One', *Library Review* (Glasgow),
XXII, No. 8 (Winter 1970) 442–443. [Review article.]
Osaka, Osamu, 'Some Critical Notes on Brendan Behan – With Special
Reference to His Plays', *Studies in English Literature and Language*
(Fukuoka, Japan: Kyushu University), XXIV (1974) 79–104. [In
Japanese; summary in English, 161–162.]
——, 'Critical Notes on Brendan Behan (2): The Making of *The Quare
Fellow* and Its Analysis', *Studies in English Literature and Language*
(Fukuoka, Japan: Kyushu University), XXV (1975) 45–79. [In
Japanese; summary in English, 133–136.]
Osborne, Charles, '*The Hostage*', *The London Magazine*, VI (September
1959) 90.
O'Shannon, Cathal, 'Behan in Borstal', *Evening Press* (Dublin, 24
October 1958) pp. 10, 14. [*Borstal Boy.*]
——, 'Sidelights on Brendan', *Evening Press* (Dublin, 19 March 1965)
p. 8. [Review article.]
O'Sullivan, Terry, 'Last Farewell', *Evening Press* (Dublin, 21 March
1964) p. 11. [Tribute to Behan.]
——, 'Brendan Behan Drank Here', *The Irish Digest* (Dublin),
LXXXVI, No. 1 (March 1966) 11–14. [Recollections of Behan.]
'Other New Novels', *The Times Literary Supplement* (London, 24
November 1966) p. 1104. [*The Scarperer.*]
'Out-of-Work Behan Now Busy Singing', *The Toronto Daily Star*, (24
March 1961) p. 33. [Behan arrested in Toronto on charges of
assault and causing a disturbance.]
Page, Malcolm, 'Brendan', *Modern Drama*, XIV, No. 4 (February
1972) 485–486. [Review article.]
Paris, Jean, 'Un Otage, Interview de Jean Paris', *Cahiers Renaud-
Barrault*, No. 37: *Le Théâtre Irlandais*, (February 1962) 54–65.

Partially published as 'Un Dramaturge engagé: Brendan Behan', *Le Nouveau Journal* (Montreal), Supplément Littéraire, (14 October 1961) pp. 5–6. [*The Hostage*.]

Payne, Basil, 'Two Hard Men', *The Irish Times* (Dublin, 8 December 1962) p. 10. [Review article.]

Pearson, Greg, 'Irish Playwright Avoids "Gargle": Brendan Behan Captivates Tijuana Gathering', *The San Diego Union*, (11 June 1961) p. 31. [Interview with Behan.]

'Pen and Gab', *The Times Literary Supplement*, (12 October 1962) p. 791. [*Brendan Behan's Island*.]

'Pendennis', 'Poet or Drunkard', *The Observer* (London, 1 April 1979) p. 9. [Brian Behan to write biography of his mother, Kathleen.]

Perley, Marie E., 'Behan's Story Ends Too Soon, Too', *The Louisville Times*, (19 November 1964) Section 1, p. 13. [*Brendan Behan's New York*.]

Perrott, Roy, 'The Man Inside Brendan Behan', *The Observer* (London, 22 March 1964) p. 3. [Appreciations by Joan Littlewood, Frank Norman, Peter Brook, Sean O'Casey, and Maurice Richardson.]

Peterborough, 'Miss Littlewood's Part', *The Daily Telegraph* (London, 21 March 1964) p. 8. [*The Quare Fellow*.]

Pharos, 'A Spectator's Notebook', *The Spectator* (London, 14 November 1958) p. 635. [*Borstal Boy*.]

Phelps, Corey, 'Borstal Revisited', *I Carb S* (Carbondale, Illinois: Friends of Morris Library, Southern Illinois Library), II (Winter–Spring 1975) 39–60. [Manuscripts and evolution of *Borstal Boy*.]

Phillips, McCandlish, 'Brandt of Berlin to Review St. Patrick's Parade–Behan Uninvited', *The New York Times*, (16 March 1961) p. 16. [The Parade Committee pronounces Behan unwelcome.]

Phillips, Philip, 'Mr. Behan Himself–The Quare Fellow', *Daily Herald* (London, 19 June 1956) p. 1. [Behan's drunken appearance on BBC TV, interviewed by Malcolm Muggeridge.]

Pitman, Robert, 'Mr. Behan of Dublin Makes the Potted Plants Shake', *The Sunday Express* (London, 12 October 1958) p. 6. [Interview with Behan.]

——, 'The Genteel Muse Who Keeps Mr. Behan Working', *The Sunday Express* (London, 5 January 1964) p. 6. [Interview with Rae Jeffs, who edited Behan's later works.]

'Playwright Fined 5s.', *The Times* (London, 13 July 1959) p. 4. [For being drunk in London.]

'Playwright Gravely Ill', *Irish Independent* (Dublin, 16 March 1964) p. 1. [In Dublin hospital.]

'Playwright in a Coma', *Irish Independent* (Dublin, 18 March 1964) p. 1. [In Dublin hospital.]

'Playwright Is Semi-Conscious; Brendan Behan Injuries Mystery', *Evening Herald* (Dublin, 30 December 1963) p. 1. [Behan found lying on roadway in Dublin.]

'Playwright Was Nervous on TV', *The Daily Telegraph* (London, 19 June 1956) p. 8. [Behan's drunken appearance on BBC TV, interviewed by Malcolm Muggeridge.]

'Playwright's Epigrams Delight Students', *Belfast News-Letter*, (31 October 1956) p. 6. [Report on Behan's talk, 'H. M. Prisons Today', to Literary and Scientific Society at Queen's University, Belfast.]

'Poet of the Pubs', *Newsweek* (New York), LXIII (29 June 1964) 89. [*The Scarperer.*]

Poirot-Delpech, B., 'Brendan Behan Est Mort', *Le Monde* (Paris, 22–23 March 1964) p. 18. [Obituary.]

Poore, Charles, 'Books of the Times', *The New York Times*, (23 October 1962) p. 35. [*Brendan Behan's Island.*]

——, 'Ireland's Iconoclast Behan Roves His Native Land in Unusual Tome', *St. Petersburg Times* (Florida, 4 November 1962) p. 15. [*Brendan Behan's Island.*]

——, 'In the World of Dublin and Brendan Behan', *The New York Times*, (28 January 1964) p. 29. [*Hold Your Hour and Have Another.*]

——, 'Brendan Behan's Pop Art, Police-Romance Escapade', *The New York Times*, (23 June 1964) p. 31. [*The Scarperer.*]

[Portrait and Quotation by Behan], *Maclean's* (Toronto), LXXXVII, No. 11 (November 1974) 102.

Powell, Arnold, 'Behan Comments on Many Things', *Birmingham News* (Alabama, 25 November 1962) p. E-7 [*Brendan Behan's Island.*]

Powell, Violet, 'The Return of the Hostage', *Punch* (London), CCXLIII (17 October 1962) 576. [*Brendan Behan's Island.*]

Preger, Janie, 'Brendan', *The Guardian* (London, 6 March 1965) p. 5. [Recollections of Behan.]

Prescott, Orville, 'Books of the Times', *The New York Times* (27 February 1959) p. 23. [*Borstal Boy.*]

'Prison Playwright', *Plays and Players* (London), III, No. 10 (July 1956) 16. [Biographical note.]

'Problems That Confront the New Abbey Theatre', *The Irish Digest*, LXXVIII, No. 4 (October 1963) 79–83. [Behan and other Irish-born playwrights have little or no connection with the Abbey.].

Pryce-Jones, Alan, 'Hullabaloo', *Theatre Arts* (New York), XLIV

(November 1960) 8–9. [*The Hostage.*]

——, 'Wheezy Behan Humor', *New York Herald Tribune*, (28 January 1964) p. 19. [*Hold Your Hour and Have Another.*]

'A "Quare Fellow" on TV Puzzles Viewers', *Belfast Telegraph*, (19 June 1956) p. 6. [Behan's drunken appearance on BBC TV, interviewed by Malcolm Muggeridge.]

'*The Quare Fellow*', *The Irish Times* (Dublin, 17 November 1956) p. 6. [The text issued in book form.]

Quidnunc, 'An Irishman's Diary: Approved', *The Irish Times* (Dublin, 21 July 1956) p. 8. [Seamus Byrne's play *Design for a Headstone* is a prison play like Behan's *The Quare Fellow.*]

——, 'An Irishman's Diary', *The Irish Times* (Dublin, 4 April 1959) p. 5. [Behan in Paris.]

——, 'An Irishman's Diary: London Burns, Behan Roams', *The Irish Times* (Dublin, 15 June 1959) p. 6. [Behan in Connemara after success of *The Hostage* in London.]

——, 'An Irishman's Diary', *The Irish Times* (Dublin, 24 March 1964) p. 9. [*The Scarperer.*]

——, 'An Irishman's Diary: Gill on Behan', *The Irish Times* (Dublin, 22 April 1970) p. 11. [*Borstal Boy* adaptation for the stage.]

——, 'An Irish Man's Diary', *The Irish Times* (Dublin, 9 March 1974) p. 11. [A plaque for Behan at 14 Russell Street, Dublin, where he was reared.]

Quigly, Isabel, 'The Chase in View', *The Spectator* (London), CCXVII (18 November 1966) 657. [*The Scarperer.*]

Quill, Gynter, ' "Confessions of an Irish Rebel" Takes Up After "Borstal Boy" ', *Waco Tribune Herald* (28 May 1966) p. 11A. [*Confessions of an Irish Rebel.*]

Quinlan, James, 'Brendan Behan's Posthumous Book Becomes Testament', *Pittsburgh Catholic*, (23 November 1966) p. 5. [*Confessions of an Irish Rebel.*]

R., T., 'One Manhattan', *Chicago Daily News*, (7 November 1964). [*Brendan Behan's New York.*]

Raffles, Gerald, 'A British People's Theatre: Theatre Workshop', *International Theatre Annual* (London), No. 3 (1958) 167–179. [*The Quare Fellow*, passim.]

Rafroidi, Patrick, 'La Scène Littéraire Irlandaise Contemporaine', *Les Langues Modernes*, II (March 1967) 84–89 passim.

Rahill, Frank, ' "The Borstal Boy" Grows Up', *Milwaukee Journal*, (15 May 1966) part 5, p. 4. [*Confessions of an Irish Rebel.*]

Randall, W. J., 'An Irishman's View of Borstal Life', *The Catholic*

Herald (London, 21 November 1958) p. 3. [*Borstal Boy.*]

'Rebel for a Cause', *The Times Literary Supplement*, (24 October 1958) p. 606. [*Borstal Boy.*]

Redmond, T., 'Irish Odyssey', *The Irish Democrat* (London, January 1963) 7. [*Brendan Behan's Island.*]

——, 'Behan's N.Y.', *The Irish Democrat* (London, February 1965) 7. [*Brendan Behan's New York.*]

Retherford, James, 'Behan's Confessions Show "Almost" Genius', *The Indianapolis Star*, (24 July 1966) Section 7, p. 5. [*Confessions of an Irish Rebel.*]

Reynolds, Horace, 'Behan's "Scarperer"', *The Christian Science Monitor* (Boston, 18 June 1964) p. 7. [Review article.]

'*Richard's Cork Leg*', *British Book News* (London, November 1973) 761.

'*Richard's Cork Leg* by Brendan Behan', *The Amateur Stage* (London), XXVIII (November 1973) 50.

Richardson, Maurice, 'Television', *The Observer* (London, 24 June 1956) p. 8. [Behan's drunken appearance on BBC TV, interviewed by Malcolm Muggeridge.]

——, 'Young Prisoners', *The Observer* (London, 19 October 1958) p. 21. [*Borstal Boy.*]

——, 'Deckhand on Collier', *The Observer* (London, 22 March 1964) p. 3. [Recollections of Behan.]

——, 'Behan on Tape', *The Observer* (London, 7 November 1965) p. 27. [*Confessions of an Irish Rebel.*]

——, 'Beatrice and Brendan', *The Observer* (London, 10 February 1974) p. 33. [Review article.]

Richman, Charles, 'Behan', *Brooklyn Record*, (6 May 1966). [*Confessions of an Irish Rebel.*]

Ricks, Christopher, 'Bee-Keeper', *New York Review of Books*, II (20 July 1964) pp. 8–9. [*The Scarperer* and *Hold Your Hour and Have Another.*]

Riordan, Liam, 'A Genius – Or a Great Talent?', *The Irish Catholic* (Dublin, 2 April 1964) p. 5. [Tribute to Behan.]

Robbins, Jhan, and June Robbins, 'Beatrice and Brendan Behan: Love Remembered', *Redbook Magazine* (Dayton, Ohio), CXXVI (March 1966) 60, 103–110. [Recollections of Behan.]

Roberts, George, 'Books', *Columbus Citizen-Journal* (Ohio, 7 November 1964) Section 2, p. 1. [*Brendan Behan's New York.*]

Robinson, Liam, 'The Great Adventure of Being Mrs. Behan', *The Irish Digest* (Dublin), LXXI, No. 5 (November 1962) 15–18. [Interview with Beatrice Behan, Behan's wife.]

——, 'The Behan I Knew Was a Man of Three Faces', *The Sunday Express* (London, 22 March 1964) p. 8. [Recollections of Behan.]

Robinson, Robert, ' "You Deserve to Be Hung," Said Mr. Behan', *Sunday Graphic* (London, 15 July 1956) p. 13. [Interview with Behan.]

Rodgers, W. R., 'Downstarts', *New Statesman* (London), LXIV (12 October 1962) 492. [*Brendan Behan's Island.*]

——, 'A Behan Rag-Bag', *The Sunday Times* (London, 15 September 1963) p. 30. [*Hold Your Hour and Have Another.*]

——, 'Salute to Brendan Behan', *The Sunday Times* (London 22 March 1964) p. 35. [Tribute to Behan.]

Rollins, Ronald G., 'O'Casey, Yeats and Behan: A Prismatic View of the 1916 Easter Week Rising', *The Sean O'Casey Review*, II, No. 2 (Spring 1976) 196–207. [*The Hostage.*]

Rooney, Philip, 'Behan: The Lonely Borstal Prisoner', *The Irish Press* (Dublin, 25 October 1958) p. 4. [*Borstal Boy.*]

Ross, Don, 'Brendan Behan Here for His Play', *New York Herald Tribune*, (3 September 1960) pp. 1, 7. [Interview with Behan.]

Rushe, Desmond, 'First Play Was His Greatest', *Irish Independent* (Dublin, 21 March 1964) p. 14. [Tribute to Behan.]

——, 'Behan on Tape', *Irish Independent* (Dublin, 13 November 1965) p. 9. [*Confessions of an Irish Rebel.*]

Russell, Arnold, 'CTV Brendan Was a Two-Pint Man', *Reynolds News* (London, 22 July 1956) p. 1. [Behan interviewed by Clifford Davis for 'Show Talk'.]

Russell, Francis, 'Dublin in the Doldrums', *The National Review* (New York), XVI (July 1964) 612–617. [Recollections of Behan.]

Ryan, Desmond F., 'Letter from Paris: Welcome to Another B. B.', *The Irish Times* (Dublin, 9 April 1959) p. 8. [*The Hostage* in Paris.]

Ryan, Stephen P., 'Crisis in Irish Letters; Literary Life in Dublin', *Commonweal* (New York), LXXI (18 December 1959), 347–349. [Behan is mentioned as 'the sort of literary "character" who yarns up in Dublin at regular intervals'.]

——, 'Ireland and Its Writers', *Catholic World*, XCII (December 1960) 149–155. [Complaints against the influence of the Church and the sterility of Irish society, by Behan and others.]

——, 'Brendan Behan: *Hold Your Hour and Have Another*', *Best Sellers* (Scranton, Pennsylvania), XXIII (1 February 1964) 383.

——, '*Hold Your Hour and Have Another*', *The Critic* (Chicago), XXII (February 1964) 80.

Ryan, Stephen P., 'Brendan Behan: *The Scarperer*', *Best Sellers*
(Scranton, Pennsylvania), XXIV (1 July 1964) 137.
——, 'Dominic Behan: *My Brother Brendan*', *Best Sellers* (Scranton,
Pennsylvania), XXVI (1 April 1966) 2. [Review article.]
——, 'Brendan Behan: *Confessions of an Irish Rebel*', *Best Sellers*
(Scranton, Pennsylvania), XXVI (1 June 1966) 94.
Rye, Jack A., 'Behan's Irish and Plot Twist Are Amusing', *Sacramento
Bee*, (5 July 1964) p. 16. [*The Scarperer*.]
S., P., 'He Loved the Whole Human Race', *Evening Herald* (Dublin, 21
March 1964) p. 3. [Tribute to Behan.]
——, ' "Greatest City" of Them All', *The Fayette Observer*, (8
November 1964) p. 5D. [*Brendan Behan's New York*.]
——, 'Behan's First Play', *The Times* (London, 15 July 1970) p. 8.
[Part of *The Landlady* manuscript found.]
——, 'Huston Hostage', *The Times* (London, 27 November 1970)
p. 10. [*The Hostage* to be filmed.]
S., W. G., 'Borstal Boy', *Books and Bookmen* (London), IV (November
1958) 13.
'A Sad Story', *The Sunday Press* (Dublin, 3 March 1974) p. 23.
[Review article.]
Schier, Ernie, 'That "Wild" Irish Playwright', *The Sunday Bulletin*
(Philadelphia, 13 November 1960) p. 7. [Biographical sketch.]
Schultz, Howard, 'Full Tour of Ireland with Behan', *Richmond Times
Dispatch* (Virginia, 18 November 1962) p. L11 [*Brendan Behan's
Island*.]
'Scrudu ar Bhreandan O Beachain', *Inniu* (Dublin, 29 July 1977) p. 5.
[Review article.]
Shackleton, Edith, 'New Books', *The Lady* (London), CLVIII (26
September 1963) 418. [*Hold Your Hour and Have Another*.]
Shaw, Iain, 'The Fire Goes Out', *Tribune* (London, 27 March 1964)
p. 13. [Tribute to Behan.]
Sheridan, Martin, 'Within the Gates', *The Irish Times* (Dublin, 25
October 1958) p. 6. [*Borstal Boy*.]
Sherman, John K., 'A Wild Irish Rogue Tells of Jails, Binges,
Writing', *Minneapolis Sunday Tribune*, (22 May 1966) Section E,
p. 6. [*Confessions of an Irish Rebel*.]
Shorey, Kenneth Paul, 'Theater Workshop: "A British People's
Theatre" ', *Modern Age* (Chicago), V (1961) 407–412. [Includes
discussion of *The Quare Fellow* and *The Hostage*.]
Shrapnel, Norman, 'Brendan on the Quiet', *Manchester Guardian
Weekly*, (24 November 1966) p. 11. [*The Scarperer*.]

Sieradzka-Grymínska, Teresa, 'Brendan Behan's *Confessions of an Irish Rebel* – A Sample of Anglo-Irish Novelized Autobiography', *Zagadnienia Rodzajów Literackich*, XVII, No. 1 (1974) 49–64. ['The everlasting value of Behan's autobiographical methods mainly arises from the author's fidelity at describing "a slice of real life".'.]

Simpson, Leo, 'Brendan, Boy, Just Wait'll They Get You Home!', *The Telegram* (Toronto, 22 March 1961) p. 7. [A jaundiced view of Behan.]

Smith, Goldie Capers, 'Irresponsible Rebel', *Tulsa Sunday World*, (10 July 1966) p. 15. [*Confessions of an Irish Rebel*.]

Smith, Gus, 'Plays Made Him World Famous', *Sunday Independent* (Dublin, 22 March 1964) p. 7. [Appreciation of Behan.]

Smith, Miles A., 'Another of Behan's Monologues', *Augusta Chronicle* (Georgia, 8 November 1964) p. 14E. [*Brendan's Behan's New York*.]

Smith, Paul, 'Dublin's Lusty Theatre', *Holiday* (Philadelphia), XXXIII (April 1963) 119ff. [Behan is a 'playwright very much of the Dublin scene today, but of neither literary nor any real theatrical importance'.]

Sokolyans'kii, M., 'Serditii smikh Brendana Biena [The Angry Laughter of Brendan Behan]', *Vsesvit* (Kiev), X (1967) 112–115.

'A Sorry Morning for Mr. Behan; TV Playwright "Didn't Really Mean To Get Drunk"', *Daily Express* (London, 20 June 1956) p. 9. [Behan's drunken appearance on BBC TV, interviewed by Malcolm Muggeridge.]

Sparrow, Bonita, 'Behan Drained Life to Dregs', *Memphis Commercial Appeal*, (19 June 1966) Section 5, p. 8. [*Confessions of an Irish Rebel*.]

Spearman, Walter, 'Behan's New York', *Rocky Mount Sunday Telegram* (North Carolina, 6 December 1964) p. 5B. [*Brendan Behan's New York*.]

'Spontaneity on U.S. Television', *The Times* (London, 10 November 1959) p. 12. [Behan on Edward R. Murrow's 'Small World' show.]

'Squibs Greet Mr. Behan at Q. U. B.', *Irish Press* (Dublin, 31 October 1956) p. 5. [Report on Behan's talk, 'H. M. Prisons Today', to Literary and Scientific Society at Queen's University, Belfast.]

'Stage World Pays Playwright Tribute', *The Irish Times* (Dublin, 21 March 1964), pp. 1, 9. [Contributions by Sean O'Casey, Ernest Blythe, Carolyn Swift, Micheal O hAodha, and Rae Jeffs.]

'Star Lights Go Up In Lr. Parnell Street', *Evening Press* (Dublin, 3

December 1958) p. 12. [Behan switches on Christmas fairylights.]

Starkie, Walter, 'Irish Extravaganza', *Saturday Review* (New York), XLIII (12 March 1960) 84. [Review article.]

Stem, Thad, Jr., 'Behan: "Look, Ma, No Hands"', *Charlotte Observer* (North Carolina, 28 October 1962) p. 5E [*Brendan Behan's Island*.]

Stuart, Francis, 'A New Spirit', *The Irish Press* (Dublin, 4 April 1964) p. 6. [Tribute to and recollections of Behan.]

Styan, J. L., 'The Published Play after 1956', *British Book News*, CCC (August 1965) 521–525. [Behan and John Osborne have been successful in fusing protest themes with new dramatic techniques.]

'Such a Strange TV Interview', *Daily Mirror* (London, 19 June 1956) p. 24. [Behan's drunken appearance on BBC TV, interviewed by Malcolm Muggeridge.]

Sullivan, A. M., 'In Durance Vile, and Later', *Saturday Review* (New York), XLII (28 February 1959) 35. [*Borstal Boy*.]

——, 'The Side Streets of Dublin', *Saturday Review* (New York), XLVII (8 February 1964) 39–40. [*Hold Your Hour and Have Another*.]

Sullivan, Kevin, 'Last Playboy of the Western World', *The Nation* (New York), CC (15 March 1965) 283–287. [Evaluation of Behan.]

Sullivan, Richard, '*The Scarperer*', *Books Today* (*Chicago Tribune*, 21 June 1964) p. 6.

Sutton, Horace, 'Recalling the Borstal Boy', *Saturday Review* (New York), L (2 December 1967) 48–49. [Review article.]

Swann, Caroline, 'There's No Place on Earth Like the World!' *Theatre Arts* (New York), XLVI (November 1962) 26–27. [Recollections of Behan by the coproducer of the Broadway production of *The Hostage*.]

Sweeney, Anne, 'Irishman's Reflections on Manhattan Unique', *Nashville Banner*, (18 December 1964). [*Brendan Behan's New York*.]

Swift, Carolyn, 'The Pike; Four Dubliners and an Idea', *Encore* (London), III, No. 3 (Summer 1956) 11–12. [The story of the Pike Theatre, Dublin, where *The Quare Fellow* had its world premiere.]

——, 'Enthralled', *The Irish Times* (Dublin, 21 March 1964) p. 1. [Tribute to Behan.]

——, 'Play Doctors', *The Irish Times* (Dublin, 12 October 1967) p. 9. [Letter to the Editor on *The Quare Fellow*.]

Sylvester, Max, 'I Can Stop Brendan Drinking', *The Irish Digest* (Dublin), LXXVIII, No. 2 (August 1963) 76. [Recollections of Behan.]

'Talk of the Town: Defiant Appearance', *Glasgow Evening News*, (19 June 1956) p. 4. [Behan's drunken appearance on BBC TV interviewed by Malcolm Muggeridge.]

Tanfield, Paul, 'A Man and His Habits', *Daily Mail* (London, 12 September 1958) p. 12. [Interview with Behan.]

Tauber, Herbert, 'Brendan Behan – Exzentriker und Dichter', *Die Weltwoche* (Zurich, 13 February 1959) p. 5. [Behan as an eccentric and as a poet.]

Taylor, John Russell, 'British Drama of the Fifties', *World Theatre*, XI, No. 3 (Autumn 1962) 241–254. Reprinted in *On Contemporary Literature; An Anthology of Critical Essays on the Major Movements and Writers of Contemporary Literature*, ed. Richard Kostelanetz (New York: Avon Books, 1964) pp. 90–96 passim.

'Tears as Behan is Laid to Rest', *The Irish Press* (Dublin, 24 March 1964) p. 7.

'Telegrams in Brief: Canberra', *The Times* (London, 20 November 1958) p. 11. [*Borstal Boy* banned in Australia.]

'There's No Hope For Brendan – Mother', *Toronto Daily Star*, (22 March 1961) p. 8. [Interview in Dublin with Kathleen Behan, Brendan's mother.]

Thomas, Leslie, 'She Drove Brendan to Drink . . . Milk', *The Evening News and Star*, (6 May 1965) p. 4C. [Recollections of Behan.]

Thomas, Mike, 'Brendan Behan Sips Seltzer at Fishermen's Wharf', *Monterey Peninsula Herald*, (15 May 1961) p. 5. [Interview with Behan.]

Thomas, Robert J., 'Books for Vermonters', *Rutland Daily Herald* (Vermont, 23 October 1962) p. 8. [*Brendan Behan's Island*.]

Thompson, Francis J., 'Exuberant Observations of a Bibulous Irishman', *Tampa Tribune*, (13 January 1963) p. 33 [*Brendan Behan's Island*.]

——, 'Wild Irish Prose', *The Tampa Tribune*, (3 July 1966) p. 31. [*Confessions of an Irish Rebel*.]

Thompson, Marjorie, 'The Image of Youth in the Contemporary Theater', *Modern Drama*, VII, No. 4 (February 1965) 433–445. [In Behan and others.]

Thomson, Hugh, 'Improvisation Taken Too Far in New Revue', *The Globe and Mail* (Toronto, 21 March 1961) p. 9. [Behan's revue

'Impulse!' at the O'Keefe Centre, Toronto.]
'The Thumb in the Stew', *Time* (Chicago), LXXXVII (3 June 1966) 98. [Review article.]
'Tippler on Television', *Newsweek*, XLVIII (2 July 1956) 70. [Behan's drunken appearance on BBC TV, interviewed by Malcolm Muggeridge.]
' 'Tis a Quare Tale Now', *Daily Sketch* (London, 20 June 1956) p. 16. [Behan's drunken appearance on BBC TV, interviewed by Malcolm Muggeridge.]
'To Hell with Everybody', *Books and Bookmen* (London), IV (November 1958) 13. [Interview with Behan.]
Todd, Olivier, '"Un Peuple Partisan" de Brendan Behan', *France Observateur*, (22 December 1960) 21. [*Borstal Boy*.]
Trilling, Ossia, 'The Young British Drama', *Modern Drama*, III, No. 2 (September 1960) pp. 168–177. [Behan and others.]
———, 'The New English Realism', *Tulane Drama Review*, VII, No. 2 (Winter 1962) 184–193. [The element of revolt in Behan and others.]
Turner, Don, 'We Did Brendan Proud', *Daily Mail* (London, 24 March 1964) p. 11. [Behan mourned in Dublin.]
' 'Twas a Nippy Parade, and a Day for Nipping', *Daily News* (New York, 18 March 1961) p. 5. [Behan invited to St. Patrick's Day Parade in Jersey City.]
'U.S. Tribute to Behan', *Evening Herald* (Dublin, 21 March 1964) p. 1.
Van Vliet, James, 'Outspoken Irishman Ends Montreal Visit', *Montreal Star*, (14 December 1960) p. 3. [Interview with Behan.]
W., C. M., 'Brendan Behan', *The Hollins Critic* (Hollins College, Virginia), II, No. 1 (February 1965) 5. [Biographical note.]
W.-E., R., 'Brendan Behan', *Books and Bookmen* (London, October 1962) 39. [*Brendan Behan's Island*.]
Wain, John, 'The Artist as a Young Delinquent', *New York Times Book Review*, (22 February 1959) pp. 1, 14. [*Borstal Boy*.]
Walker, James Robert, 'Irisches Zeugnis: Brendan Behan', *Merkur*, XVIII (1964) 691–696. [Appreciation of Behan.]
Walker, Larry, 'Behan's Island: Caustic, Funny', *Oklahoman* (Oklahoma City, Oklahoma, 30 December 1962) p. 3D. [*Brendan Behan's Island*.]
Walker, Peregrine, 'Out of Prison', *The Tablet* (London, 25 October 1958) 360–361. [*Borstal Boy*.]
Wall, Richard, '*An Giall* and *The Hostage* Compared', *Modern Drama*,

XVIII, No. 2 (June 1975) 165–172.

——, 'The Major Works of Brendan Behan', *Modern Drama*, XVIII, No. 2 (June 1975) 213–214. [Review article.]

Wardle, Irving, 'New Waves on the British Stage', *Plays and Players* (London), XI, No. 1 (October 1963) 12–14. [Behan and other new dramatists.]

——, 'The Quare Fellow', *The Observer* (London, 22 March 1964) p. 24. [Tribute to Behan.]

'Warrant Out for Behan', *The New York Times*, (28 March 1961) p. 39. [Issued for the arrest of Behan when he did not appear in court on charges of assault and causing a disturbance in Toronto.]

Watson, John, 'Seein' Behan Is Believin'', *New York Journal-American*, (13 November 1960) p. 43. [Interview with Behan.]

'We Can't Turn Out a Yeats Every Week', *Evening Press* (Dublin), (6 May 1959) p. 6 [Interview with Behan.]

'We Don't Have Leprehauns, Paddys and Magic Mists', *Newsweek*, (27 March 1961) 28. [Interview with Behan.]

Weatherby, W. J., 'But Not in the Pejorative Sense', *The Guardian* (London, 4 March 1960) p. 9. [Interview with Behan.]

Weintraub, Stanley, 'To Dublin in a Donkey Cart', *Saturday Review* (New York), IL (4 June 1966) 47. [Review article.]

——, 'Brendan Behan', *Books Abroad*, XLI (1967) 227–228. [*Confessions of an Irish Rebel*.]

Weldon, Oliver, 'Everybody Gets It in That Last Behan Play', *The Sunday Press* (Dublin, 29 March 1964) p. 27. [*Richard's Cork Leg*.]

White, Jack, 'Vintage Behan', *The Irish Times* (Dublin, 12 November 1966) p. 8. [*The Scarperer*.]

White, Terence de Vere, 'B & I', *The Irish Times* (Dublin, 29 September 1962) p. 8. [*Brendan Behan's Island*.]

White, W. J., 'Brendan Behan's Boswell', *Manchester Guardian Weekly* (18 November 1965) p. 10. [*Confessions of an Irish Rebel*.]

Whittington-Egan, Richard, 'Biography', *Books and Bookmen* (London), XI (December 1965) 29. [Review article.]

'Who Lives Here?' *Evening Press* (Dublin, 10 January 1964) pp. 1, 3. [Behan in Meath Hospital, Dublin.]

Wickstrom, Gordon M., 'The Heroic Dimension in Brendan Behan's *The Hostage*', *Educational Theatre Journal*, XXII (1970) 406–411.

'"Wild One" Brendan Behan Dies at 41', *Daily Mirror* (London, 21 March 1964), p. 1.

'Will This Be Behan's Best?' *Evening Press* (Dublin, 21 March 1964) p. 9. [*The Scarperer*.]

Wilson, Angus, 'New Playwrights', *Partisan Review* (New York), XXVI (Fall 1959) 631–634. [Behan is mentioned as a more famous representative of the new movement than any other playwright.]

Wilson, Georges, 'Un Cri!' *Les Lettres Françaises*, No. 1022 (26 March–1 April 1964) p. 8. [Recollections of Behan.]

Wilson, Madge, 'An Irishman's View From His Pub', *Daily Press* (Virginia, 2 December 1962) p. 4D. [*Brendan Behan's Island.*]

Wilson, W. A., 'Behan Talks "Freely" during McGill Visit', *The Montreal Star*, (9 December 1960) p. 3. [Report on a lecture at Moyse Hall, McGill University.]

Winch, Terence, 'My Life with Brendan', *New Letters* (Kansas City: University of Missouri), XLII (Fall 1975) 115–116. [Review article.]

Winocour, Jack, 'Behan's Last Night Out in London', *Picture Post* (London, 30 June 1956) pp. 6–9. [Behan's drunken appearance on BBC TV, interviewed by Malcolm Muggeridge.]

Winston, Carl, 'Behan Got Around', *San Francisco News Call Bulletin*, (7 November 1964) p. 7. [*Brendan Behan's New York.*]

Wolfe, Ann F., 'Macabre Suspense in Behan's Only Novel', *Columbus Dispatch* (Ohio, 5 July 1964) p. 12. [*The Scarperer.*]

Women Stand in City Streets Weeping', *Sunday Press* (Dublin), (22 March 1964) p. 6. [Behan's funeral.]

'World-Wide Tributes to Behan's Genius', *The Irish Press* (Dublin, 21 March 1964) p. 3. [By Sean O'Casey, Ernest Blythe, Micheal O hAodha, Carolyn Swift, and Rae Jeffs.]

'A Wreath for Brendan Behan', *The Irish Digest*, LXXX, No. 3 (May 1964) 81–84. [Excerpts from obituaries by Joan Littlewood, Benedict Kiely, Alan Brien, Seamus Kelly, Gus Smith, Liam Riordan, W. R. Rodgers, Flann O'Brien, and Liam Robinson.]

'Writer Fined £2 on Drink Charge', *The Irish Press* (Dublin, 7 March 1959) p. 9. [In Bray, near Dublin.]

Zara, Louis, 'Poet Behind the Mask of a Clown', *Saturday Review* (New York), LI (13 April 1968) 43. [Review article.]

Ziemba, Ronald S., '*Brendan Behan's New York*: Irish Poet's Final Book', *The Springfield Republican*, (15 November 1964) p. 4D.

C) Reviews of Play Productions, including Dramatisations and Films Based on Behan's Life or His Works, as well as News of Productions.

[This section is arranged chronologically under each title]

THE QUARE FELLOW

'*The Quare Fellow* at the Pike', *The Irish Times* (Dublin, 20 November 1954) p. 9. [Presented by Alan Simpson at the Pike Theatre, Dublin, 19 November 1954.]

R[obinson], L[ennox], 'Acting Was Superb in Behan Play', *The Irish Press* (Dublin, 20 November 1954) p. 9.

Fallon, Gabriel, 'Behan's Play Should Not Be Missed', *Evening Press* (Dublin, 20 November 1954) p. 3.

F., J., 'Last Night's New Play: Song Instead of Curtain Speech', *Evening Herald* (Dublin, 20 November 1954) p. 6.

F., R. M., 'Prison Strike at Pike', *Dublin Evening Mail*, (20 November 1954) p. 6.

L., N., 'Premiere of Play by New Dramatist', *Irish Independent* (Dublin, 22 November 1954) p. 2.

Leventhal, A. J., 'Dramatic commentary: *The Quare Fellow* by Brendan Behan. The Pike Theatre Club', *The Dublin Magazine*, XXI, No. 1 (January–March 1955) 47–48.

Carthew, Anthony, 'An Irishman Finds His Oasis', *Daily Herald* (London, 18 May 1956) p. 8.

'London Diary: Behan Attempts a Coup de Theatre', *The Northern Whig* (Belfast, 23 May 1956) p. 2.

'Theatre Workshop to Introduce Brendan Behan', *The Stage* (London, 24 May 1956) pp. 1, 13.

'Theatre Workshop: *The Quare Fellow*', *The Times* (London, 25 May 1956) p. 3. [At the Theatre Royal, Stratford East, London, 24 May 1956.]

Darlington, W. A., 'An Irish Prison Play', *The Daily Telegraph* (London, 25 May 1956) p. 11.

'A Very Unusual First Night', *The Daily Mail* (London, 25 May 1956) p. 3.

Barber, John, 'A Hangman Calls – A Jail Waits', *Daily Express*
    (London, 25 May 1956) p. 7.
Nathan, David, 'The Inside Story of the Final Drop', *Daily Herald*
    (London, 25 May 1956) p. 5.
Frank, Elizabeth, 'Condemned Man Does Not Appear', *News Chronicle*
    (London, 25 May 1956) p. 3.
Wraight, Robert, 'Quare Fellow & "The Job"', *The Star* (London, 25
    May 1956) p. 3.
Tynan, Kenneth, 'The End of the Noose', *The Observer* (London, 25
    May 1956) p. 11.
'Gala Night at Theatre Royal', *Stratford Express*, (25 May 1956) p. 2.
    [News item.]
Rowe, James, 'Drama Review: Condemned Cell', *Walthamstow
    Guardian*, (25 May 1956) p. 13.
'Irish Author's Play', *Irish Independent* (Dublin, 25 May 1956) p. 10.
'Behan Play Praised in London', *Evening Press* (Dublin, 25 May 1956)
    p. 5.
'Tragedy with Laughs', *Manchester Guardian*, (26 May 1956) p. 4.
Fisher, Desmond, 'Behan Play Pleased Critics, House', *The Irish Press*
    (Dublin, 26 May 1956) p. 6.
'London Diary: Brendan Causes Novel Rising', *The Northern Whig*
    (Belfast, 26 May 1956) p. 2.
Driberg, Tom, 'The French Step Out', *Reynolds News* (London, 27
    May 1956) p. 6.
Grahame, Paul, 'In the Shadow of the Rope', *Daily Worker* (London,
    28 May 1956) p. 2.
'Against Capital Punishment', *The Stage* (London, 31 May 1956) 10.
I., B., '*The Quare Fellow* by Brendan Behan', *The Spectator* (London),
    CXCVI (1 June 1956) 761.
'Theatre: The Quare Fellow', *The Jewish Chronicle* (London, 1 June
    1956) p. 24.
Levin, Bernard, '*The Quare Fellow*: Theatre Royal, Stratford, E. 15',
    Truth (London), CLVI (1 June 1956) 639.
Lally, G., 'A Play about Hanging – That Doesn't Preach', *Stratford
    Express*, (1 June 1956) p. 5.
Rowe, James, 'Lawful Killing', *Walthamstow Guardian*, (1 June 1956)
    p. 13.
Hutten, Kenneth A., 'Theatre', *What's on in London* (1 June 1956) p. 7.
Richardson, Maurice, 'O'Casey Goes to Jail', *New Statesman* (London),
    LI (2 June 1956) 624.
Gomm, Ted, 'A Socialist at the Theatre: *The Quare Fellow*', *The*

Socialist Leader (Glasgow, 2 June 1956) p. 2.

Boorne, Bill, 'Show News: Off My Cuff', *Evening News* (London, 2 June 1956) p. 6. [Offers for filming of *The Quare Fellow* by four companies.]

Findlater, Richard, 'Waiting for the Hangman', *The Tribune* (London, 8 June 1956) p. 8.

McC[all], C[olin], 'Theatre: Tales of Two Capitals', *The Freethinker* (London), LXXVI, No. 23 (8 June 1956) 187–188.

Cain, Alex Matheson, 'Death's Jest Book', *The Tablet* (London), CCVII (9 June 1956) 540.

'Versatile Acting from Maxwell Shaw', *East End News* (London, 15 June 1956) p. 3.

'*The Quare Fellow* Comes West', *Evening Standard* (London, 29 June 1956) p. 7. [To be presented at the Comedy Theatre, London.]

Grahame, Paul, '*The Quare Fellow* Comes to West End', *Daily Worker* (London, 30 June 1956) p. 2.

'"Quare Fellow"', *News Chronicle* (London, 30 June 1956) p. 3. [To have a West End run.]

'*The Quare Fellow* at Stratford', *The Irish Democrat* (London, June 1956) p. 6.

'*The Quare Fellow*', *The Stage* (London, 5 July 1956) p. 8. [To open at the Comedy Theatre on 24 July.]

'*The Quare Fellow*', *Evening Argus* (Brighton, 6 July 1956) p. 8.

'*The Quare Fellow* Is Coming', *Brighton & Hove Gazette* (7 July 1956) p. 12.

'Irish Prison Play for New York', *Evening Herald* (Dublin, 9 July 1956) p. 5.

'*The Quare Fellow*', *The Times* (London, 10 July 1956) p. 14. [To be produced in New York.]

'Brendan Behan's Play for New York', *The Irish Times* (Dublin, 10 July 1956) p. 7. [In the autumn, by David Ross.]

'"Quare Fella" for New York Stage', *The Irish Press* (Dublin, 10 July 1956) p. 1. [Rights acquired by David Ross.]

'Theatre Royal, Brighton', *West Sussex County Times* (Horsham, 13 July 1956) p. 4.

'Next Week's Shows', *Brighton and Hove Herald*, (14 July 1956) p. 5.

'No Hanging Play at Brighton', *Eastbourne Herald Chronicle*, (14 July 1956) p. 16.

'U. S. Producer's Acclaim for Playwright Behan', *The Irish Press* (Dublin, 16 July 1956) p. 11. [David Ross on Broadway plans for the play's production.]

V., M. D., 'To Be Hanged by the Neck', *Evening Argus* (Brighton, 17 July 1956) p. 4. [At the Theatre Royal, Brighton, 16 July 1956.]

'Around the Shows: Theatre Royal – Brighton', *Mid-Sussex Times*, (18 July 1956) p. 10.

C., J., ' "The Quare Fellow" Is a Brilliant Cascade', *Southern Weekly News* (Brighton, 20 July 1956) p. 11.

Viney, Michael, 'You Never Can Tell with Brendan', *Evening Argus* (Brighton, 20 July 1956) p. 8.

'London Letter: Rehearsing in Brighton', *Irish Independent* (Dublin, 20 July 1956) p. 10.

Ingham, C. W., 'Next Week in the Theatre: Prison Play by Man Who Was Inside', *The Star* (London, 21 July 1956) p. 5.

'London Letter: Theatre Nights', *Birmingham Post*, (21 July 1956) p. 6.

Hobman, Molly, 'London Theatre: Voice of Youth', *Oxford Mail*, (21 July 1956) p. 4.

C., N., 'The Last Breakfast', *Brighton and Hove Herald*, (21 July 1956) p. 5.

'Brendan Behan on Television Tonight', *The Irish Times* (Dublin, 21 July 1956) p. 1. [On the Independent Television programme 'Show Talk' to discuss *The Quare Fellow*.]

Glass, Ian, 'Visiting London', *Daily Express* (London, 24 July 1956) p. 6.

'Mr. Manchester's Diary: That Man Again', *Manchester Evening News*, (24 July 1956) p. 4.

'*The Quare Fellow*: Mr. Brendan Behan's Play at Comedy Theatre', *The Times* (London, 25 July 1956) p. 5. [At the Comedy Theatre, London, 24 July 1956.]

Granger, Derek, 'Comedy Theatre: *The Quare Fellow*', *The Financial Times* (London, 25 July 1956) p. 2.

Gibbs, Patrick, 'Comedy – Drama of a Hanging: *The Quare Fellow*', *The Daily Telegraph* (London, 25 July 1956) p. 8.

Conway, Harold, 'Fun for the Quare Fellow', *Daily Sketch* (London, 25 July 1956) p. 4.

Barber, John, 'The Two Dramas of Irishman Behan', *Daily Express* (London, 25 July 1956) p. 7.

Carthew, Anthony, 'I Say, Old Behan', *Daily Herald* (London, 25 July 1956) p. 3.

Tee, Robert, 'It's Quare – But Successful', *Daily Mirror* (London, 25 July 1956) p. 15.

Wilson, Cecil, 'Again the Quare Fellow Triumphs', *Daily Mail* (London, 25 July 1956) p. 3.

Dent, Alan, 'Prison Play: *The Quare Fellow*', *News Chronicle* (London, 25 July 1956) p. 3.

I[ngham], C. W., 'A Comment on Hanging', *The Star* (London, 25 July 1956) p. 3.

Shulman, Milton, 'Mr. Behan Spares No Ghoulish Detail', *Evening Standard* (London, 25 July 1956) p. 6.

Williams, Stephen, 'If Only This Was a Play', *Evening News* (London, 25 July 1956) p. 3. [In Edition B only.]

'Behan Play Received with Enthusiasm in West End', *Irish Press* (Dublin, 25 July 1956) p. 5.

' "Quare Fellow" Opens: Behan's Play Is Cheered at Theatre in London', *The New York Times*, (25 July 1956) p. 24.

T[rewin], J. C., '*The Quare Fellow* at the Comedy Theatre', *Birmingham Post*, (26 July 1956) p. 5.

'London Diary: Quarer and Quarer', *The Northern Whig* (Belfast, 26 July 1956) p. 2.

Hope-Wallace, Philip, 'Brendan Behan's *Quare Fellow*', *Manchester Guardian*, (27 July 1956) p. 5.

'Our London Letter: Before the Execution', *Western Morning News*, (Plymouth, 27 July 1956) p. 4.

Walker, Roy, 'At the Theatre', *The Observer* (London, 29 July 1956) p. 10.

Hobson, Harold, 'The Pity of It', *The Sunday Times* (London, 29 July 1956) p. 4.

Monsey, Derek, 'Sordid – But Exciting', *Sunday Express* (London, 29 July 1956) p. 9.

'Theatre: *The Quare Fellow* (Comedy)', *Sunday Dispatch* (London, 29 July 1956) p. 8.

Jackson, Frank, 'New Author Gives West End Stiffness a Jolt', *Reynolds News* (London, 29 July 1956) p. 7.

'The New Shows: *The Quare Fellow* (Comedy)', *Sunday Graphic* (London, 29 July 1956) p. 13.

Shepherd, Ross, 'London Shows: *The Quare Fellow* (Comedy)', *The People* (London, 29 July 1956) p. 4.

'The London Theatres: Shades of the Prison House', *Western Independent* (Plymouth, 29 July 1956) p. 16.

Grahame, Paul, 'Theatre', *Daily Worker* (London, 30 July 1956) p. 2.

B., F. G., '*The Quare Fellow*', *Plays and Players* (London), III, No. 10 (July 1956) 29.

M., H. G., '*The Quare Fellow* (Theatre Royal, Stratford, E.)', *Theatre World* (London), LII (July 1956) 5.

Keown, Eric, '*The Quare Fellow* (Comedy)', *Punch* (London), CCXXXI
(1 August 1956) 139–140.

S., C., '*The Quare Fellow*', *The Stage* (London, 2 August 1956) p. 9.

Scott, George, '*The Quare Fellow*: Comedy', *Truth* (London), CLVI (3
August 1956) 900–901.

Trewin, J. C., 'The New Plays: *The Quare Fellow* (Comedy)', *The Lady*
(London), CXLIV (9 August 1956) 201.

Simon, Clare, 'The Hours Before Execution', *The Catholic Herald*
(London, 10 August 1956) p. 3.

Trewin, J. C., 'Through Irish Eyes', *The Illustrated London News*,
CCXXIX (11 August 1956) 238.

Heaven, Sidney, '*The Quare Fellow*', *Plays and Players* (London), III,
No. 12 (September 1956) 16–17.

'*The Quare Fella* at the Abbey Theatre', *The Irish Times* (Dublin, 9
October 1956) p. 3. [At the Abbey Theatre, Dublin, 8 October
1956.]

M., I., 'Prison Life Drama', *Irish Independent* (Dublin, 9 October 1956)
p. 8.

'Brendan Behan's "Fatted Calf"',*The Irish Press* (Dublin, 9 October
1956) p. 6.

Fallon, Gabriel, 'The Makings of a Masterpiece', *Evening Press*
(Dublin, 9 October 1956) p. 4.

F[inegan], J. J., 'Prison Drama at the Abbey', *Evening Herald* (Dublin,
9 October 1956) p. 5.

Fox, R. M., 'Best Abbey Play for Long Time', *Dublin Evening Mail*, (9
October 1956) p. 6.

'"The Quare Fellow" To be Produced in Belfast', *Belfast News-Letter*,
(31 October 1956) p. 6. [At the Group Theatre.]

'*The Quare Fellow* Given Overwhelming Reception', *Belfast News-Letter*,
(28 November 1956) p. 3. [At the Group Theatre, Belfast, 27
November 1956.]

'Group Theatre, Belfast: *The Quare Fellow* Earns "Approved" Verdict',
The Northern Whig (Belfast, 28 November 1956) p. 5.

H., J., 'Behan Play in Belfast', *The Irish Times* (Dublin, 29 November
1956) p. 11.

Olden, G. A., '*The Quare Fella*', *The Irish Times* (Dublin, 8 December
1956) p. 8. [Broadcast on Radio Eireann.]

Lambert, J. W., 'Plays in Performance', *Drama* (London), No. 43
(Winter 1956) 22.

'*The Quare Fellow* on Television', *The Times* (London, 6 November
1958) p. 3. [Associated-Rediffusion.]

Atkinson, Brooks, 'Theatre: "Quare Fellow"', *The New York Times*, (28 November 1958) p. 34. [At the Circle-in-the-Square Theatre, New York, 27 November 1958.]

Crist, Judith, '"Quare Fellow" Presented at Circle-in-the-Square', *New York Herald Tribune*, (28 November 1958) p. 14.

McLean, John, '*The Quare Fellow*', *Journal American* (New York), (28 November 1958) p. 18.

Jess, 'Off-Broadway Reviews: The Quare Fellow', *Variety*, (3 December 1958) 89.

Malcolm, Donald, 'Off Broadway: An Objection Sustained', *New Yorker*, XXXIV (6 December 1958) 123–124.

'New Plays in Manhattan', *Time*, LXXII (8 December 1958) 79–80.

'Theater: Black Irishman's Mood', *Newsweek*, LII (8 December 1958) 66–67.

Hewes, Henry, 'Broadway Postscript: The Quare World of Brendan Behan', *Saturday Review* (New York), XLI (13 December 1958) 27–28.

'*The Quare Fellow*', *Vogue*, CXXXIII (1 January 1959) 95, 146.

Clurman, Harold. 'Theatre', *The Nation* (New York), CLXXXVIII (3 January 1959) 20.

Hayes, Richard, 'The Irish Presence', *Commonweal*, LXIX (23 January 1959) 438–439.

Savery, Ranald, 'Echoes from Broadway', *Theatre World* (London), LV (January 1959) 46.

'Off Broadway: The Quare Fellow', *Theatre Arts* (New York), XLIII (February 1959) 66.

Wyatt, Euphemia Van Rensselaer, '*The Quare Fellow*', *Catholic World*, CLXXXVIII (February 1959) 420.

'*The Quare Fellow* in Berlin', *The Times* (London, 16 March 1959) p. 3.

Luft, Friedrich, '*Behans Mann von L morgen früh*', *Die Welt* (Berlin, 16 March 1959) p. 5. [At the Schillertheater, Berlin.]

'Behans Jag beginnt mit Whisky', *Bild Zeitung* (Berlin), (16 March 1959) p. 3.

Mando, 'Schillertheater: Behan–Premiere', *B. Z.* (Berlin), (16 March 1959) p. 9.

Gassner, John, 'Broadway in Review', *Educational Theatre Journal* XI, No. 1 (March 1959) 29–39.

'Un Irlandais à Paris', *Paris-Presse l'Intransigeant*, (3 April 1959) p. 2F [To be presented in Paris.]

B., Ph., ' "Very Good" a dit Brendan Behan', *Le Figaro* (Paris, 16 April 1959) p. 18. [To be presented in Paris under the title *Le Client du Matin*.]

Gautier, Jean-Jacques, 'A L'Œuvre: *Le Client du Matin* de Brendan Behan', *Le Figaro* (Paris, 17 April 1959) p. 18. [At Théâtre de l'Œuvre, Paris.]

Leclerc, Guy, 'Au Théâtre de l'Œuvre', *L'Humanité* (Paris, 17 April 1959) p. 2.

Gordeaux, Paul, 'Au Théâtre de l'Œuvre: *Le Client du Matin*', *France-Soir*, (17 April 1959) p. 8.

Maulnier, Thierry, 'Le Client du Matin au Théâtre de l'Œuvre', *Combat* (Paris, 17 April 1959) p. 2.

'*Le Client du Matin* de Brendan Behan: Une Prison et un condamné à mort', *France Observateur* (Paris, 16 April 1959) p. 24.

Berger, Pierre, '*Le Client du Matin* de Behan', *Paris-Journal*, (20 April 1959) p. 6.

Marcel, Gabriel, 'Le Théâtre', *Les Nouvelles littéraires* (Paris, 30 April 1959) p. 10.

Hutchinson, Pearse, 'Truth by the Gallows-Tree', *Hibernia* (Dublin), XXIV (26 August 1960) 7. [At the Abbey Theatre, Dublin.]

'This Wasn't "The Quare Fella"!', *Sunday Independent* (Dublin, 23 September 1962) p. 5. [The World premiere of the film *The Quare Fellow* at the Cork Film Festival.]

'The Shadow of the Condemned Cell. Rialto Cinema: *The Quare Fellow*', *The Times* (London, 5 October 1962) p. 18. [The film version, directed by Arthur Dreifus, shown in London.]

Coleman, John, 'Colour Problems', *New Statesman* (London), LXIV (5 October 1962) 465–466.

Cameron, Ian, 'Movies on Show', *The Spectator* (London, 12 October 1962) p. 560.

Dent, Alan, 'Quare and Notorious', *The Illustrated London News*, CCXLI (27 October 1962) 672.

Durgnat, Raymond, '*The Quare Fellow*', *Films and Filming* (London), IX (November 1962) 34.

Selznick, Daniel, 'Movie Review: *The Quare Fellow*', *The New York Standard*, (22 February 1963) p. 10. [At the Carnegie Hall Cinema.]

'Cinema: A Hanging Matter – *The Quare Fellow*', *Time*, International Edition, LXXXI (8 March 1963) 69.

Hill, Ronald, '*The Quare Fellow*: Playhouse, Liverpool', *Theatre World* (London), LX (November 1964) 32.

THE BIG HOUSE

'New Behan Play at the Pike', *The Irish Times* (Dublin, 15 April 1958)
p. 9. [At the Pike Theatre, Dublin, 14 April 1958.]

M., I., 'Pike Theatre Re-opens with Two Premieres', *Irish Independent*
(Dublin, 15 April 1958) p. 10.

'Double Bill At Pike', *The Irish Press* (Dublin, 15 April 1958) p. 2.
[With Sartre's *Men with Shadows*.]

F[inegan], J. J., 'Tragedy and Comedy in Pike's Twin Bill', *Evening
Herald* (Dublin, 15 April 1958) p. 4.

Fallon, Gabriel, 'Behan Play Opens at the Pike', *Evening Press* (Dublin,
15 April 1958) p. 4.

F., R. M., 'Gay and Tragic Plays at the Pike', *Dublin Evening Mail*,
(15 April 1958) p. 6.

'Double Bill', *The Sunday Press* (Dublin, 20 April 1958) p. 16.

'Mr. Behan Back in Ribald Mood: Theatre Royal Stratford, E.', *The
Times* (London, 30 July 1963) p. 13.

Worsley, T. C., 'Theatre Royal, Stratford, E.: Three Irish Plays', *The
Financial Times* (London, 30 July 1963) p. 18.

Kenyon, Michael, 'Festival of Irish Comedy', *The Guardian* (London,
30 July 1963) p. 7.

Darlington, W. A., 'Irish Plays Fail to Inspire', *The Daily Telegraph*
(London, 30 July 1963) p. 12.

Nathan, David, 'Brendan Saves the Irish', *Daily Herald* (London, 30
July 1963) p. 5.

Shulman, Milton, 'A Drop of Irish, but the Flavour Is Weak', *Evening
Standard* (London, 30 July 1963) p. 4.

Barker, Felix, 'A Drop of the Irish', *Evening News* (London, 30 July
1963) p. 3.

D., P., 'Behan Broadside', *Daily Worker* (London, 31 July 1963) p. 2.

Marriott, R. B., 'At Stratford East: Irish Comedy with Synge and
Behan', *The Stage* (London, 1 August 1963) p. 7.

Tynan, Kenneth, 'Dubliners in the East End', *The Observer* (London, 4
August 1963) p. 17.

Hobson, Harold, 'Theatre', *The Sunday Times* (London, 4 August
1963) p. 25.

Brien, Alan, 'Theatre', *The Sunday Telegraph* (London, 4 August 1963)
p. 8.

Gellert, Roger, 'O'Booze', *New Statesman* (London), LXVI (9 August
1963) 178.

Shaw, Iain, 'The Pike at Stratford', *Tribune* (London, 9 August 1963) p. 7.

Trewin, J. C., 'The World of the Theatre', *The Illustrated London News* (10 August 1963) 216.

——, 'The New Plays', *The Lady* (London), CLVIII (15 August 1963) 201.

Pryce-Jones, David, 'Old Pike', *The Spectator* (London, 16 August 1963) 205.

Taylor, John Russell, '*The Big House*', *Plays and Players* (London), XL, No. 1 (October 1963) 42.

Lambert, J. W., 'Plays in Performance', *Drama* (London), No. 71 (Winter 1963) 22.

THE NEW HOUSE [Combined title for *Moving Out* and *The Garden Party*].

'Pike: *The New House* by Brendan Behan', *The Irish Times* (Dublin, 6 May 1958) p. 9. [In a double bill with *The Big House*.]

O'H., M., 'Behan Journeys to Back of Beyond', *The Irish Press* (Dublin, 6 May 1958) p. 2.

O'B., C., 'New Behan Play at the Pike', *Evening Press* (Dublin, 6 May 1958) p. 4.

B., P. F., '*The New House*', *Evening Herald* (Dublin, 6 May 1958) p. 4.

F., R. M., Full Marks for Comedy Element', *Dublin Evening Mail*, (6 May 1958) p. 6.

L., N., 'New Company at Pike Theatre', *Irish Independent* (Dublin, 7 May 1958) p. 12.

THE HOSTAGE

'Brendan Behan's Fine Play in Irish', *The Irish Times* (Dublin, 17 June 1958) p. 8. [Presented by An Club Drámaíochta, under the auspices of Gael-Linn, at the Damer Hall, Dublin, 16 June 1958.]

S., R., 'New Irish Play Begins at Damer Hall', *Irish Independent* (Dublin, 17 June 1958) p. 8.

O'D., M., 'Moradh na Daonnachta an tAor', *The Irish Press* (Dublin, 17 June 1958) p. 11.

B., P. F., 'New Behan Play', *Evening Herald* (Dublin, 17 June 1958)
p. 3.

T., L., 'New Behan Play Is Best Yet', *Evening Press* (Dublin, 17 June
1958) p. 6.

S., F., 'Over the Footlights', *Theatre World* (London), LIV (October
1958) 7. [After several months of doubt and uncertainty following
the withdrawl of some of their grants, Theatre Workshop are to
re-open the Theatre Royal, Stratford, London E.15, on 14
October 1958 with *The Hostage*.]

'Good Talkers All; Mr. Brendan Behan's Extravaganza', *The Times*
(London, 15 October 1958) p. 8. [Presented by Theatre
Workshop at the Theatre Royal, Stratford East, London, 14
October 1958.]

Worsley, T. C., 'Theatre Royal, Stratford, E.: *The Hostage*', *Financial
Times* (London, 15 October 1958) p. 15.

Coton, A. V., 'Shades of Sean O'Casey: Tragi-Comedy of Irish
Politics', *Daily Telegraph* (London, 15 October 1958) p. 10.

Goring, Edward, 'It's Screwy, Says Behan and That Sums It Up',
Daily Mail (London, 15 October 1958) p. 3.

Carthew, Anthony, 'Behan Is So Good – and So Bad', *Daily Herald*
(London, 15 October 1958) p. 3.

Richards, Dick, 'B. B. Takes the Mickey out of the Trouble', *Daily
Mirror* (London, 15 October 1958) p. 16.

Barber, John, 'I'd Just Hate to Tie Down Mr. Behan, But–', *Daily
Express* (London, 15 October 1958) p. 9.

Dent, Alan, 'Behan Makes a Broth of a Play', *News Chronicle* (London,
15 October 1958) p. 3.

Shulman, Milton, 'Mr. Behan Makes Fun of the IRA', *Evening
Standard* (London, 15 October 1958) p. 13.

Hope-Wallace, Philip, 'Brendan Behan's *The Hostage*: O'Casey-cum-
Brecht', *The Manchester Guardian*, (16 October 1958) p. 7.

S., L. G., 'Irish Play Is Nearly Great', *The Stage* (London, 16 October
1958) p. 12.

Brien, Alan, 'Political Pantomime', *The Spectator* (London), CCI (17
October 1958) 513–514.

Tynan, Kenneth, 'New Amalgam', *The Observer* (London, 19 October
1958) p. 19.

Hobson, Harold, 'Triumph at Stratford East', *Sunday Times* (London,
19 October 1958) p. 21.

'The New Shows: *The Hostage* (Theatre Royal, Stratford East)', *Sunday
Graphic* (London, 19 October 1958) p. 20.

Jackson, Frank, 'Theatre', *Reynolds News* (London, 19 October 1958) p. 7.

'Behan's Big Night: *The Hostage* (Theatre Workshop)', *The People* (London, 19 October 1958) p. 17.

Keown, Eric, '*The Hostage* (Theatre Royal, Stratford)', *Punch* (London), CCXXXV (22 October 1958) 543–544.

Jones, Mervyn, 'The Master of Farce', *Tribune* (London, 24 October 1958) p. 11.

Robinson, Robert, 'The Square Fella', *New Statesman* (London), LVI (25 October 1958) 560.

Cain, Alex Matheson, 'Plays and Non-Plays', *The Tablet* (London, 25 October 1958) 352.

Gomm, Ted, '*The Hostage*: Theatre Royal, Stratford E.', *The Socialist Leader* (Glasgow, 25 October 1958) p. 2.

'Brendan Triumphs Again', *The Sunday Press* (Dublin, 26 October 1958) p. 15.

Trewin, J. C., 'The New Plays: *The Hostage* (Theatre Royal, Stratford, E.)', *The Lady* (London), CXLVIII (30 October 1958) 541.

——, 'Go-As-You-Please', *The Illustrated London News*, CCXXXIII (1 November 1958) 764.

Friedenthal, Richard, 'Tanz, Liebe, Getränke, leichte Mädchen', *Welt* (Berlin, 7 November 1958) p. 9.

Gilliatt, Penelope, 'Brendan Beano', *Encore* (London), V, No. 4 (November 1958) 35–36.

M., H. G., 'Theatre Royal, Stratford E.: *The Hostage*', *Theatre World* (London), LIV (November 1958) 8, 38.

Smith, Lisa Gordon, '*The Hostage*', *Plays and Players* (London), VI, No. 3 (December 1958) 17.

Lambert, J. W., 'Plays in Performance', *Drama* (London), No. 51 (Winter 1958) 18.

Aubry, Jacques, 'Paris Découvre un Auteur Neuf', *Paris-Journal*, (28–29 March 1959) p. 6.

'Un Irlandais à Paris', *Paris-Presse l'Intransigeant*, (3 April 1959) p. 2F.

Mallory, Leslie, 'Mr. Behan Gets Full Diplomatic Recognition After All', *News Chronicle* (London, 4 April 1959) p. 1. [As the British entry at the Paris Théâtre des Nations Festival, 3 April 1959.]

Tanfield, Paul, 'A Taste of Paris', *Daily Mail* (London, 4 April 1959) p. 12.

Bouvard, Philippe, 'Rires et Sourires, Hier au Théâtre des Nations', *Le Figaro* (Paris, 4–5 April 1959) p. 12.

Gordeaux, Paul, 'Au Théâtre des Nations: The Hostage de Brendan
Behan', *France-Soir*, (5–6 April 1959) p. 9.
Lerminier, Georges, 'Le Workshop dans *L'Otage* de Brendan Behan',
Le Parisien, (6 April 1959) p. 6.
Jamet, Dominique, 'The Hostage au Théâtre des Nations', *Combat*
(Paris, 6 April 1959) p. 2.
Joly, G., 'Triomphe du Workshop de Londres dans *The Hostage*',
L'Aurope, (6 April 1959) p. 4a.
'Paris Triumph for *The Hostage*', *The Times* (London, 6 April 1959)
p. 3.
Merlin, Olivier, 'Au Théâtre des Nations: *The Hostage* par le
Workshop de Londres', *Le Monde* (Paris, 8 April 1959) p. 12.
Kasters, Robert, '*The Hostage* du Théâtre Fair-Play', *L'Express* (Paris, 9
April 1959) p. 36.
M., L., '*The Hostage* de Brendan Behan', *France Observateur*, (9 April
1959) p. 21.
Marcorelles, Louis, 'Un Nouveau Théâtre Anglais', *France Observateur*,
(9 April 1959) p. 21.
Lemarchand, Jacques 'Au Théâtre des Nations: Théâtre Workshop –
The Hostage', *Le Figaro Littéraire* (Paris, 11 April 1959) p. 16.
Trilling, Ossia, 'The International Scene', *Theatre World* (London), LV
(May 1959) 41.
'An Extravaganza with Roaring Vitality', *The Times* (London, 12
June 1959) p. 15. [At the Wyndham's Theatre, London, 11 June
1959.]
Worsley, T. C., 'Wyndham's Theatre: *The Hostage*', *The Financial
Times* (London, 12 June 1959) p. 19.
Darlington, W. A., 'Mr. Behan Charms Away the Grimness', *Daily
Telegraph* (London, 12 June 1959) p. 14.
Wilson, Cecil, 'Slapstick, Sentiment and Satire', *Daily Mail* (London,
12 June 1959) p. 3.
Thompson, John, 'Get Ready for Shocks at Behan's New Play', *Daily
Express* (London, 12 June 1959) p. 6.
Richards, Dick, 'A Rather Seedy Affair', *Daily Mirror* (London, 12
June 1959) p. 16.
Dent, Alan, 'A Taste of Poteen – and What a Kick', *News Chronicle*
(London, 12 June 1959) p. 3.
Wraight, Robert, 'A Perishin' Broth of a Frolic', *The Star* (London, 12
June 1959) p. 17.
Shulman, Milton, 'Mr. Behan Has Fun with His IRA Heroes', *Evening
Standard* (London, 12 June 1959) p. 6.

Barker, Felix, 'It's Bedlam with Behan!', *Evening News* (London, 12 June 1959) p. 7.

Fay, Gerard, '*Hostage* Shows an Immense Improvement', *The Manchester Guardian*, (13 June 1959) p. 5.

'London Letter: *The Hostage*', *The Irish Times* (Dublin, 13 June 1959) p. 7.

Jones, Mervyn, 'No Boos for Brendan', *The Observer* (London, 14 June 1959) p. 25.

Hobson, Harold, 'Theatre: *The Hostage*', *The Sunday Times* (London, 14 June 1959) p. 23.

Monsey, Derek, 'Behan Offers an Irish Stew', *The Sunday Express* (London, 14 June 1959) p. 17.

'At the Theatre', *Sunday Dispatch* (London, 14 June 1959) p. 7.

Jackson, Frank, 'New Shows', *Reynolds News* (London, 14 June 1959) p. 7.

M., R. B., 'Humour and Humanity of *The Hostage* – In Town at Last', *The Stage* (London, 18 June 1959) p. 11.

Young, Elizabeth, 'Theatre', *Tribune* (London, 19 June 1959) p. 11.

Trewin, J. C., 'The New Plays: *The Hostage* (Wyndham's)', *The Lady* (London), CXLIX (25 June 1959) 946.

Cain, Alex Matheson, 'French Without Laughs', *The Tablet* (London, 27 June 1959) 573.

'Behan Gets into Act at London Theatre', *The New York Times*, (10 July 1959) p. 28.

Buckle, Richard, 'Keep Britain Black', *Plays and Players*, (London), VI, No. 11 (August 1959), 13.

S., F., 'Wyndham's: *The Hostage*', *Theatre World* (London), LV (August 1959) 7. See also pictures, 20–21.

C., W. D., 'Disestablishmentarianism', *The Twentieth Century* (London), CLXVI (September 1959) 174–175.

'Princess Amused by Naughty Play', *The Evening Sun* (Baltimore, 24 November 1959) p. 3. [Princess Margaret.]

Lambert, J. W., 'Plays in Performance', *Drama* (London), No. 55 (Winter 1959) 18.

M., C. M., 'Glasgow Theatres: High Humour with Critical Undertones', *The Glasgow Herald* (16 August 1960) p. 8. [At the King's Theatre, Glasgow.] See correspondence by George N. Scott, ibid., (18 August 1960) p. 6; by C. M. M., ibid., (19 August 1960) p. 8; by Geraint V. Jones, ibid., (20 August 1960) p. 6; by Clarence Wilkie and D. H. Stewart, ibid., (22 August 1960) p. 6; by John Griffin and W. C. Watson, ibid., (23 August

1960) p. 6; by C. M. M., ibid., (24 August 1960) p. 6; by
F. W. M. Bennett, Jean Mann, and Richard Holloway, ibid., (25
August 1960) p. 6; and by John Griffin, ibid., (26 August 1960)
p. 6.

Taubman, Howard, 'Behan Buffoonery: *The Hostage* Makes Debut at
the Cort', *The New York Times*, (21 September 1960) p. 42.
[Produced by Leonard S. Field and Caroline Burke Swann at the
Cort Theatre, New York, 20 September 1960.]

Watts, Richard, Jr., 'The Exuberance of Brendan Behan', *New York
Post*, (21 September 1960) p. 32.

Gilbert, Justin, 'Behan's 'Hostage' Earthy, Ludicrous', *New York
Mirror*, (21 September 1960) p. 27.

Chapman, John, 'In Behan's *The Hostage* There's No Such Thing as a
Little Gaelic', *Daily News* (New York, 21 September 1960) p. 55.

McClain, John, 'Not Even Mr. Behan Rolled in the Aisles', *Journal
American* (New York, 21 September 1960) p. 21.

Aston, Frank, ' "Hostage" Breaks Rules, But It Is Enchanting', *New
York World-Telegram*, (21 September 1960) p. 23.

Kerr, Walter, 'First Night Report: "The Hostage" ', *New York Herald
Tribune*, (21 September 1960) p. 18.

McCarten, John, 'Gaelic Gyrations', *New Yorker*, XXXVI (1 October
1960) 128.

Taubman, Howard, 'Laughing Boy: Behan Pokes Fun at Many
Things', *The New York Times*, (2 October 1960) Section 2, p. 1.

'New Play on Broadway', *Time* (Chicago), LXXVI (3 October
1960) 59.

Brustein, Robert, 'Libido at Large', *The New Republic*, CXLIII (3
October 1960) 20–21.

'First Night: Woolly and Wonderful', *Newsweek*, LVI (3 October
1960) 57.

Hewes, Henry, 'Brendan Behan's Soup', *Saturday Review* (New York),
XLIII (8 October 1960) 32.

Clurman, Harold, 'Theatre', *The Nation* (New York), CXCI (8
October 1960) 236.

Lewis, Theophilus, 'Theatre', *America*, CIV (22 October 1960) 130.

Taubman, Howard, 'Profits of Sin', *The New York Times*, (30 October
1960) Section 2, p. 1.

Mannes, Marya, 'A Taste of Zany', *The Reporter* (New York), XXIII
(24 November 1960) 45.

Pryce-Jones, Alan, 'Hullabaloo and Strindberg Too', *Theatre Arts* (New
York), XLIV (November 1960) 8–9.

Ryan, Stephen P., '*The Hostage*', *The Catholic World* (New York), XCII (November 1960) 126–127.

Savery, Ranald, 'Echoes from Broadway', *Theatre World* (London), LVI (November 1960) 24.

'Behan Play Ending Run', *The New York Times*, (21 December 1960) p. 36. [To close on 7 January 1961.]

Johnson, W. Gerald, 'Brendan Behan's "Hostage" Imported from London Stage', *The Hartford Times*, (28 December 1960) p. 30.

Gelb, Arthur, '*Hostage* Switch Asked of Equity', *The New York Times*, (28 December 1960) p. 20. [Producers ask Equity to keep the play off-Broadway.]

Simon, John, 'Theatre Chronicle', *Hudson Review*, XIII, No. 4 (Winter 1960–61) 587–588.

'*The Hostage*', *New York Theatre Critics' Reviews*, XXI (1960) pp. 239–242.

Jordan, John, 'Brendan Behan's *The Hostage*', *Hibernia* (Dublin), XXIV (December 1960) 25. [*An Giall* at the Abbey Theatre, Dublin.]

Esterow, Milton, 'Equity Refuses *Hostage* Switch', *The New York Times*, (4 January 1961) p. 29.

Hatch, Robert, 'The Roaring Presence of Brendan Behan', *Horizon* (New York), III (January 1961) 113–114.

Whittaker, Herbert, '*The Hostage* Provides Impudent Vaudeville', *The Globe and Mail* (Toronto, 31 January 1961) p. 9. [At the O'Keefe Centre, Toronto.]

'Spirited Company; Topical Quips in Behan Play. Lyric Opera House, Hammersmith', *The Times* (London, 14 February 1961) p. 6.

Worsley, T. C., 'Lyric, Hammersmith: *The Hostage*', *The Financial Times* (London, 14 February 1961) p. 18.

Hastings, Ronald, '*The Hostage* Roars Again – Missing Hand of Littlewood', *Daily Telegraph* (London, 14 February 1961) p. 14.

Lewis, Peter, 'Such Brawling, But It's Still Infectious', *Daily Mail* (London, 14 February 1961) p. 3.

Shulman, Milton, '*The Hostage* Takes a Lot of Killing', *Evening Standard* (London, 14 February 1961) p. 12.

Myer, Caren, '*The Hostage* – As Funny as Ever', *Evening News* (London, 14 February 1961) p. 7.

W., E., 'Theatre: *The Hostage* (Lyric, Hammersmith)', *Daily Worker* (London, 15 February 1961) p. 2.

H., P., 'Topicalities in Revival of *The Hostage*', *The Stage* (London, 16 February 1961) p. 13.

Craig, H. A. L., 'Life-Anti-Life', *New Statesman* (London), LXI (17 February 1961) 275.

Lambert, J. W., 'Theatre', *The Sunday Times* (London, 19 February 1961) p. 37.

Lewis, Jack, 'New Shows', *Reynolds News* (London, 19 February 1961) p. 7.

Roberts, Peter, '*The Hostage*', *Plays and Players* (London), VIII, No. 7 (April 1961) 15.

'Arts and Letters', *Sewanee Review*, LXIX (Spring 1961) 335–337.

Calta, Louis, 'Behan's *The Hostage*', *The New York Times*, (13 December 1961) p. 55. [At One Sheridan Square, 12 December 1961.]

Crist, Judith, 'First Night Report: *The Hostage*', *New York Herald Tribune*, (13 December 1961) p. 18.

Oliver, Edith, 'Off Broadway', *New Yorker*, XXXVII (23 December 1961) 57–58.

Gilman, Richard, 'Blanket Coverage', *The Commonweal*, LXXV (5 January 1962) 389.

Kelly, Seamus, ' "Un Otage" in Théâtre de France', *The Irish Times* (Dublin, 17 February 1962) p. 5.

Maulnier, Thierry, 'Un otage', *Revue de Paris*, (March 1962) 152–155. [At the Théâtre de France.]

Hewes, Henry, 'Broadway Postscript: Second Helpings', *Saturday Review* (New York), XLV (19 May 1962) 30.

Watts, Richard, Jr., 'Brendan Behan Goes Brightly On', *New York Post*, (6 September 1962) p. 19.

Landey, Dora, 'Time Off for *The Hostage*', *The New York Standard*, (18 February 1963) p. 14. [At the Arena Stage, 12 February 1963.]

M., H. G., '*The Hostage* at the Tower', *Theatre World* (London), LIX (April 1963) 37.

'*The Hostage* in Its Gaelic Form Is Planned for Dublin', *Evening Herald* (Dublin, 27 March 1964) p. 8.

Finegan, J. J., 'In Iceland, Too, Brendan Was Remembered', *Evening Herald* (Dublin, 4 April 1964) p. 8. [Tomas MacAnna, the Abbey producer, invited to Iceland to direct *The Hostage*.]

'*The Hostage*: Behan's Comments Coming Out Better', *Evening Press* (Dublin, 11 July 1964) p. 9. [Plans for the forthcoming 2-week production at the Gaiety Theatre, Dublin.]

K., '*The Hostage* at the Gaiety', *The Irish Times* (Dublin, 14 July 1964) p. 6. [At the Gaiety Theatre, Dublin.]

Rushe, Desmond, 'A Vastly Better Production of *The Hostage*', *Irish*

Independent (Dublin, 14 July 1964) p. 9.

W., S. J., ' "Hostage" Staged with Gusto', *The Irish Press* (Dublin), 14
    July 1964) p. 7.

F[inegan], J. J., '*The Hostage* Comes down to Earth', *Evening Herald*
    (Dublin, 14 July 1964) p. 5.

O'F., M., 'Behan Play Has Little Lustre', *Evening Press* (Dublin, 14
    July 1964) p. 3.

'Brendan Behan Is Partly Tamed', *The Times* (London, 1 October
    1964) p. 15. [At the Little Theatre Club, London.]

N., A., 'Irish Charade', *Tribune* (London, 2 October 1964) p. 14.

Gray, Ken, 'Alias *The Hostage*', *The Irish Times* (Dublin, 21 March
    1968) p. 12. [On TV.]

O'C., R., 'Peacock: Behan's Warm Humanity Is Evident in I. R. A.
    Drama', *Irish Independent* (Dublin, 11 October 1968) p. 3.

'*An Giall* le ceol', *The Irish Press* (Dublin, 11 October 1968) p. 7.

McG., P., 'Satire and Fun in *An Giall*', *Evening Herald* (Dublin, 11
    October 1968) p. 4.

Power, Richard, 'Behan Play an Easy Mixture', *Evening Press* (Dublin,
    11 October 1968) p. 5.

Rosenfeld, Ray, 'Behan Play as Burlesque in Belfast', *The Irish Times*
    (Dublin, 12 October 1968) p. 5. [At the Belfast Centre Theatre.]

Kelly, Seamus, 'Old Age Creeps Up on *The Hostage*', *The Irish Times*
    (Dublin, 29 April 1970) p. 10. [At the Abbey Theatre, Dublin, 28
    April 1970.]

Rushe, Desmond, ' "Hostage" — Too Few Grains Amid So Much
    Chaff', *Irish Independent* (Dublin, 29 April 1970) p. 26.

Boyne, Sean 'Sparkling Show of "Hostage" ', *The Irish Press* (Dublin,
    29 April 1970) p. 3.

F[inegan], J. J., 'Original Touches in Abbey "Hostage" ', *Evening
    Herald* (Dublin, 29 April 1970) p. 5.

O'Kelly, Emer, 'Behan's Hostage', *The Sunday Press* (Dublin, 3 May
    1970) p. 25.

Jordan, John, '*The Hostage*', *Hibernia* (Dublin, 15 May 1970) p. 22.
    'Players on Tour', *Evening Herald* (Dublin, 23 May 1970) p. 4.

Carson, Neil, 'The Toronto Workshop Productions: *The Hostage* Was
    Geoffrey Read's and Not Brendan Behan's', *Commentator*
    (Toronto), XV (March 1971) 19–20.

Gussow, Mel, 'Juilliard Unit Presents Behan's Timely *Hostage*', *The
    New York Times*, (12 May 1972) p. 24. [At the Juilliard School,
    Lincoln Center.]

Hunt, Albert, 'A Game No More', *New Society*, (8 June 1972) 524.

[Joan Littlewood's revival at the Theatre Royal, Stratford East.]
Barnes, Clive, 'Theatrical Curiosity of Behan's *Hostage*', *The New York Times*, (11 October 1972) p. 50. [At the Good Shepherd Faith Church, New York.]
Oliver, Edith, 'Off Broadway: Behan's Dubliners', *New Yorker*, XLVIII (21 October 1972) 76–78. [Produced by the City Centre Acting Company at the Juilliard School of Drama, New York.]
Clurman, Harold, 'Theatre', *The Nation* (New York), CCXV (30 October 1972) 410–411.

BORSTAL BOY

Kelly, Seamus, 'Abbey: The Living Theatre of Ireland', *The Irish Times* (Dublin, 11 October 1967) p. 8. [Frank McMahon's adaptation at the Abbey Theatre, 10 October 1967, during the Dublin International Theatre Festival.]
Martin, Augustine, 'A Superb Tale Superbly Told', *The Irish Press* (Dublin, 11 October 1967) p. 5.
O'Farrell, Maureen, 'Idea Works Like a Charm', *Evening Press* (Dublin, 11 October 1967) p. 3.
F[inegan], J. J., '*Borstal Boy* at the Abbey: A Triumph – This Epitaph to Brendan', *Evening Herald* (Dublin, 11 October 1967) p. 3.
Curtiss, Thomas Quinn, 'Behan "Borstal Boy" Is Staged in Dublin', *The New York Times*, (11 October 1967) p. 39.
'Dublin Critics Laud Stage "Borstal Boy"', *The New York Times*, (12 October 1967) p. 55.
Rushe, Desmond, 'Abbey: Behan Adaptation Outstanding', *Irish Independent* (Dublin, 12 October 1967) p. 6.
'Big Foreign Interest in *Borstal Boy*', *Irish Independent* (Dublin, 12 October 1967) p. 6.
Sutton, Horace, 'Recalling the Borstal Boy', *Saturday Review* (New York), L (2 December 1967) 48–49.
Roberts, Peter, and Gerald Colgan, 'Operation Survival', *Plays and Players* (London), XV, No. 3 (December 1967) 46–47.
Roberts, Peter, 'Dublin', *Plays and Players* (London), XVI, No. 3 (December 1968) 66. [At the Dublin International Theatre Festival.]
MacAnna, Tomas, 'A Broadway Diary', *The Irish Times* (Dublin, 27 March 1970) p. 12. [The charcoal portrait of Behan by LeRoy

Neiman is hung on stage at the Lyceum Theatre for the New
York production.]

Barnes, Clive, ' "Borstal Boy": Abbey Brings Story of Young Brendan
Behan', *The New York Times*, (1 April 1970) p. 38. [At the
Lyceum Theater, New York, 31 March 1970.]

Chapman, John, 'Behan's *Borstal Boy* in a Shiny Shamrock', *Daily
News* (New York, 1 April 1970) p. 82.

Gill, Brendan, 'The Theatre: Glad Tidings', *New Yorker*, XLVI (11
April 1970) 81–82.

Kerr, Walter, 'No Claim on Our Sympathy', *The New York Times*, (12
April 1970) Section 2, p. 9.

'Gift of Golden Gab', *Time* (Chicago), XCV (13 April 1970) 97.

Kroll, Jack, 'Tough Thrush', *Newsweek*, LXXV (13 April 1970) 83.

Hewes, Henry, 'Brendan and His Double', *Saturday Review* (New
York), LIII (18 April 1970) 26.

Clurman, Harold, 'Theatre', *The Nation* (New York), CCX (20 April
1970) 473.

Lewis, Theophilus, 'Theatre: *Borstal Boy*', *America* (New York), CXXII
(2 May 1970) 483–484.

Wahls, Robert, 'Footlights: No Tony for Frank', *Sunday News* (New
York, 3 May 1970) p. 2. [Interview with Frank Grimes, who
played Behan in *Borstal Boy*.)

Prideaux, Tom, 'Behan's Rowdy Ghost Returns', *Life* (Chicago),
LXVIII (22 May 1970) 16.

'*Borstal Boy* Suspending', *The New York Times*, (1 August 1970) p. 13.
[For summer.]

'Why *Borstal Boy* Ends on Broadway', *Sunday Independent* (Dublin, 2
August 1970) p. 4.

RICHARD'S CORK LEG

Kelly, Seamus, 'Brendan Behan – Dubliners Combination at Peacock',
The Irish Times (Dublin, 15 March 1972) p. 12. [At the Peacock
Theatre during the Dublin International Theatre Festival.]

MacGoris, Mary, 'Juvenile Brendan Unkind to Behan', *Irish
Independent* (Dublin, 15 March 1972) p. 7.

Marshall, Oliver, 'The Peacock: "Cork Leg" Leads a Merry Dance',
The Irish Press (Dublin, 15 March 1972) p. 7.

Finegan, J. J., 'Behan Play with Hardly a Leg to Stand On', *Evening Herald* (Dublin, 15 March 1972) p. 4.

MacLoughlin, Adrian, 'Not the Real Behan', *Evening Press* (Dublin, 15 March 1972) p. 4.

Lewsen, Charles, 'Dublin Theatre Festival', *The Times* (London, 24 March 1972) p. 13.

Manning, Mary, 'Theatre', *Hibernia* (Dublin, 31 March 1972) p. 19.

Archer, Kane, '*Richard's Cork Leg* at the Olympia', *The Irish Times* (Dublin, 31 May 1972) p. 10. [At the Olympia Theatre, Dublin, 30 May 1972.]

MacGoris, Mary, 'Return of Behan Play', *Irish Independent* (Dublin, 31 May 1972) p. 15.

'Drámaíocht le hEadhmonn MacSuibhne', *The Irish Press* (Dublin, 31 May 1972) p. 13.

Wardle, Irving, '*Richard's Cork Leg*', *The Times* (London, 20 September 1972) p. 7. [At the Royal Court Theatre, London, 19 September 1972.]

Billington, Michael, '*Richard's Cork Leg* at the Royal', *The Guardian* (London, 20 September 1972) p. 8.

Barber, John, 'Rag-Bag of Behan's Ribald Writings', *The Daily Telegraph* (London, 20 September 1972) p. 13.

Kretzmer, Herbert, 'Behan's Last Laugh – *Richard's Cork Leg*: Royal Court', *Daily Express* (London, 20 September 1972) p. 17.

Thirkell, Arthur, 'Theatre', *Daily Mirror* (London, 20 September 1972) p. 19.

Shulman, Milton, '*Richard's Cork Leg*', *Evening Standard* (London, 20 September 1972) p. 23.

Barker, Felix, '*Richard's Cork Leg*: Royal Court Theatre', *Evening News* (London, 20 September 1972) p. 11.

O'Connor, Garry, 'Royal Court: *Richard's Cork Leg*', *The Financial Times* (London, 21 September 1972) p. 3.

Sutherland, Jack, 'No Crime to be Human', *Morning Star* (London, 21 September 1972) p. 2.

Brustein, Robert, 'A Behan Celebration', *The Observer* (London, 24 September 1972) p. 36.

Hobson, Harold, 'Theatre: Worlds Apart', *The Sunday Times* (London, 24 September 1972) p. 37.

Marcus, Frank, 'Theatre: Hollow Laughter', *Sunday Telegraph* (London, 24 September 1972) p. 18.

Hirschhorn, Clive, 'Theatre', *The Sunday Express* (London, 24 September 1972) p. 23.

Kingston, Jeremy, 'Theatre', *Punch* (London), CCLXIII (27
September 1972) 427.
Mahon, Derek, 'Leisureliness', *The Listener* (London), LXXXVIII (28
September 1972) 423.
M., R. B., 'Behan Not at His Best at the Royal Court', *The Stage and
Television Today* (London, 28 September 1972) p. 17.
Nightingale, Benedict, 'Brendan with Hiccoughs', *New Statesman*
(London), LXXXIV (29 September 1972) 443.
Trussler, Simon, 'Old Tunes Before Noisy New Turns', *Tribune*
(London, 29 September 1972) p. 9.
Hurren, Kenneth, 'On Brendan and Noel', *The Spectator* (London),
CCXXIX (30 September 1972) 510.
Brookholding-Jones, Adrian, 'Theatre', *The Tablet* (London, 30
September 1972) 935.
Brien, Alan, '*Richard's Cork Leg*', *Plays and Players* (London), XX, No. 2
(November 1972) 42–43.
Lambert, J. W., 'Plays in Performance', *Drama* (London), No. 107
(Winter 1972) 22–23.
Smith, Gus, 'Theatre', *Sunday Independent* (Dublin, 15 January 1978)
p. 2. [Call for its revival.]

BRENDAN

Rushe, Desmond, 'Dublin: The Flourishing Trend of One-Man
Shows', *The New York Times*, (4 October 1971) p. 52. [At the
Peacock Theatre, Dublin. Devised by Ulick O'Connor.]

A JAR WITH BRENDAN BEHAN

Taylor, John Russell, 'Distinction Is Not Enough', *The Times*
(London, 5 October 1971) p. 17. [A Swedish 16 mm film.]

SHAY DUFFIN AS BRENDAN BEHAN

Gussow, Mel, 'Shay Duffin as Brendan Behan', *The New York Times*,
(3 January 1973) p. 50. [A one-man show based on the works of
Behan. At the Abbey Theatre, 136 East 13th Street, New York.]
'Shay Spit and Image of Brendan', *Sunday Independent* (Dublin, 21
January 1973) p. 13.

D) Dissertations on Brendan Behan

Bedell, Jeanne F., 'The New British Drama 1956–1966. A Critical
Study of Four Dramatists: John Osborne, Brendan Behan, Arnold
Wesker and John Arden', M.A., University of Richmond, 1967.
Boyle, Mary T., 'Characteristics of Comedy in Two Plays by Brendan
Behan', M.A., University of Nebraska, 1966.
Capurso, Mrs. Maria Antonietta, 'Brendan Behan: *Borstal Boy*', L.L.S.,
Universita di Bari, Italy, 1975. [In Italian.]
Gerdes, Peter René, 'The Major Works of Brendan Behan', Ph.D.,
University of Basel, 1973. [Published dissertation.]
Goodman, Judith Lea, 'Joan Littlewood and Her Theatre Workshop',
Ph.D., New York University, 1975. [Chapter VI deals with *The
Quare Fellow* and *The Hostage*.]
Grymińska, Teresa Sieradzka, 'Contemporary Anglo-Irish Novelized
Autobiography', Ph.D., University of Warsaw, 1973. [Includes
discussions of Behan, St. John Gogarty and Frank O'Connor.]
Harsch, J. H. H., 'The Curtain of Words: Dualism in the Plays of
Synge, O'Casey, Johnston, Behan and Beckett', Ph.D., Trinity
College Dublin, 1970.
Hinrichsen, Irene, 'Der Romancier als Übersetzer: Annemarie und
Heinrich Bölls Prosaübertragungen aus dem Englischen—Ein
Beitray zur Übersetzungskritik', Ph.D., University of Wuppertal,
1977 [Deals partly with Böll's translation of Behan.]
Kraft, Eugene Leo, 'Realism and Romanticism in Five Contemporary
British Dramatists', Ph.D., University of Missouri, Columbia,
1974. [Chapter III deals with Behan.]
Lanoix, Louis, 'Le Théâtre de Brendan Behan', Ph.D., Université de
Sorbonne, 1965.
Lauffet, Lisette, 'Realism and Poetry in the Works of Brendan Behan',
M.A., Université de Strasbourg, 1968.
Lyman, Kenneth Cox, 'Critical Reaction to Irish Drama on the New
York Stage: 1900–1958', Ph.D., University of Wisconsin, 1960.
[*The Quare Fellow.*]
McDaniel, George Rudolph, 'An annotated Bibliography of Brendan
Behan', M.A., University of North Carolina, Chapel Hill, 1978.
McNary, Nancy A., 'Brendan Behan: Clown', M.A. Columbia
University, 1965.
Molloy, Ione M., 'Notes on Brendan Behan's *The Hostage*, with
Introductory Chapters on Behan's Life and Works', M.A., Boston
College, 1964.

Moncada, Angelo, 'An Approach to Brendan Behan', L.L.S.
    Università decli studi di Venezia, 1972.
Oster, Yvette, 'A Major Political Problem in Modern Ireland: The
    Fight for Re-Unificaion in Brendan Behan's Work', M.A.,
    Université de Strasbourg, 1968.
Pannecoucke, Jean-Michel, 'Music and Drama: O'Casey, Behan,
    Keane', Ph.D., Université de Lille, 1970.
Pierrotin, Jean-Pierre, 'Brendan Behan', Ph.D., Université de
    Strasbourg, 1968.
Wintergerst, Marianne, 'Die Selbstdarstellung der Iren: Eine
    Untersuchung zum Modernen Anglo-Irischen Drama', Ph.D.,
    University of München, 1973. [The Irish as seen by themselves in
    the plays of Behan and others.]

E) Discography

The Quare Fellow, Spoken Word A-24.
Brendan Behan: Irish Folksongs and Ballads, Spoken Arts SA 760.
Brendan Behan on Joyce, Folkways Records FL 9826. [A lecture
    delivered before the James Joyce Society at the Gotham Book
    Mart, New York.]
The Hostage, Columbia DOL 329/DOP 729.
We Remember Brendan Behan – Our Own Dear Laughing Boy, Midnite
    Records (Ireland) AM 304. [An album of songs by Sean Og
    McKenna, Noel Carroll, and Liam Rowsome; with sleeve-notes
    by Rory Furlong, Behan's stepbrother; in memory of Brendan
    Behan.]

F) Manuscripts

Behan manuscripts are hard to come by. Many that were not destroyed have subsequently been lost. 'I don't want people reading my notes when I'm dead', Beatrice Behan quoted Brendan as saying (*My Life with Brendan*, p. 99). The present editor, however, has been able to locate the following manuscripts:

'The Black and Tans' [review article]. Complete typescript in the possession of Mrs. Beatrice Behan.

Borstal Boy [autobiographical novel]. Three manuscripts housed in the Special Collections of Morris Library, Southern Illinois University at Carbondale. Twenty-page typescript in the possession of Mrs. Beatrice Behan.

'the catacombs' [novel]. Ten-page typescript in the possession of Mrs. Beatrice Behan.

'The Execution' [short story]. Manuscript housed in the University College Library, Cork, Ireland.

'The Landlady' [play]. Two acts in longhand in the possession of Mrs. Beatrice Behan.

'The Last of Mrs. Murphy' [short story]. Complete typescript in the possession of Mrs. Beatrice Behan.

'Peadar O'Cearnaigh' [poem]. Complete typescript in the possession of Mr. Rory Furlong.

Richard's Cork Leg [play]. Almost-complete typescript in the possession of Mrs. Beatrice Behan.

'A Woman of No Standing' [short story]. Manuscript housed in the Special Collections of Morris Library, Southern Illinois University at Carbondale.

G) Letters

There are letters by Brendan Behan in the Fales Library, New York University; in the National Library of Ireland; in the Library and Museum of the Performing Arts, New York; and in the possession of Mrs. Beatrice Behan and other recipients. An edition of *The Letters of Brendan Behan* is being prepared by the present editor.

*   *   *

Index

Abbey Theatre, Dublin 25, 30, 68, 84, 86, 94, 95, 96, 97
Abbey Theatre, New York 100
Abirached, Robert 30
Adams, Cindy 30
Adelman, Irving 1
Alexander, James E. 16, 30
Alldridge, John 30
Allen, James 16, 30
Allsop, Kenneth 7, 30
Alvarez, A. 30
Anderson, Garrett 18
Anderson, Patrick 15
Anderson, Rick 12, 30
Andrews, Eamonn 33
Aragno, Riccardo 30
Archer, Kane 31, 99
Arena Stage, New York 95
Armstrong, William A. 18
Arnold, Bruce 31
Aspler, Tony 18, 31
Associated-Rediffusion Television 84
Aston, Frank 93
Atkinson, Brooks 18, 31, 85
Aubry, Jacques 90
Aynsley, Cyril 31
Ayre, Leslie 31

B., C. A. 16, 31
B., F. G. 83
B., P. F. 88, 89
B., Ph. 86
B., W. 14, 31
B.-R., G. 31
Babenko, V. G. 31
Bailey, The 26
Barber, John 80, 82, 89, 99
Barker, Felix 87, 92, 99
Barkham, John 11, 14, 32
Barnes, Clive 97, 98

Baro, Gene 8, 32
Barrett, William 12, 14, 32
Bedell, Jeanne F. 101
Behan, Beatrice (wife) 15, 18, 31, 32, 35, 36, 37, 39, 40, 45, 46, 47, 48, 49, 61, 62, 70, 104
Behan, Blanaid (daughter) 32, 41, 61
Behan, Brendan—biographies 18, 19, 26, 36, 37, 43, 58, 68, 72, 76; as a character 18, 19, 22, 43, 46, 53, 55, 56, 61, 64, 71, 75; general criticism on 19, 20, 21, 23, 24, 25, 26, 27, 28, 31, 44, 45, 48, 49, 51, 54, 55, 56, 58, 59, 63, 64, 66, 69, 71, 73, 74, 76, 77; as a dramatist 18, 23, 25, 26, 27, 28, 30, 46, 49, 50, 51, 56, 58, 60, 61, 64, 66, 68, 73, 74, 75, 76, 77, 78; alleged homosexuality 28, 32, 47, 53, 59; honoured 31, 34, 39, 40, 51, 59, 69, 74; ill 30, 33, 34, 35, 37, 38, 39, 44, 46, 50, 51, 61, 62, 63, 67, 68, 77; interviewed 30, 31, 33, 35, 36, 37, 38, 40, 41, 42, 43, 44, 45, 47, 48, 51, 54, 55, 58, 59, 60, 62, 63, 66, 67, 71, 73, 74, 75, 76, 77, 78; obituaries 19, 32, 34, 35, 37, 38, 42, 43, 45, 48, 55, 57, 61, 68, 78; on TV 31, 35, 38, 39, 44, 48, 49, 52, 56, 57, 61, 62, 67, 68, 69, 70, 71, 73, 74, 75, 76, 78, 82; recollected 18, 20, 21, 23, 24, 25, 27, 28, 30, 31, 32, 33, 35, 36, 39, 40, 41, 42, 43, 44, 45, 46, 47, 48, 49, 50, 52, 53, 54, 55, 56, 57, 58, 62, 63, 64, 65, 66, 68, 70, 71, 74, 75, 78; as a Republican 18, 28, 33, 40, 44, 65; trials and prisons 26, 32, 33, 34, 35, 37, 38, 39, 44, 63, 66, 67, 77, 78; trib-

106